AF413398

IN THE
LAMPLIGHT

IN THE
LAMPLIGHT

An Unexpected Discovery and a Conversation Through Time

Olivier Humbert

Printed in the United States of America

ISBN Hardcover: 9798330600151

Cover and Interior Design: Creative Publishing Book Design

To Susan, Matthew and Marc

Table of Contents

Félix Le Molt

Poetry, painting, the cunning sculptor's art,
the searching, the trial and error of nimble minds
have taught us, inching forward, step by step.
Thus, step by step, time lays each fact before us,
and reason lifts it to the coasts of light.
For men saw one thing clarify another
until civilization reached its highest peak.

–Lucretius
De rerum natura (On the Nature of Things), first century BCE

The Antique Desk

My mother's death brought my great-grandfather, Félix Le Molt, back to life. It was a serendipitous development. As a consequence of her passing, I became acquainted with this long-lost forgotten ancestor. The revival of my great-grandfather's spirit spurred a decade-long journey of self-reflection and learning. He became a vital part of my life, providing me with a better understanding of how to live.

In the summer of 2011, I traveled from Boston to rural New Jersey to commence, with my brother Xavier, the triage of her belongings—apportion to family and friends, sell *in situ*, or discard. I was also sorting through a tangle of emotions. The reviewing, compacting, and dissolution of my mother's world both evoked sorrow and fueled transformation.

In my mother's living room sat a nineteenth-century French ladies' writing desk—a *bonheur du jour*, or what twentieth-century Americans called a "secretary." The compact desk was made of smooth, dark, and well-crafted mahogany. As with other desks of its era, there were two parts—a leather writing area that could be folded up with a single drawer supported by fluted tapering legs, and an upper half comprised of a cabinet with a black marble shelf.

Crowning the shelf was a bronze gallery that accentuated the desk's elegance and beauty. Tambour doors locked to shield the cabinet's contents from prying eyes. My mother was a private person, and I knew that upon opening those doors I would be entering her emotional world.

The desk had two imposing sentinels. Atop the black marble shelf, a polychrome carved angel just over a foot tall stood protectively. This eighteenth-century Italian wood carving was flanked by a terra cotta bust of what appeared to be a sixteenth-century hooded monk. The man had formidable facial features, a flowing beard, and piercing eyes. He was not someone to be trifled with.

The rest of the exposed desk contained a variety of other small heirlooms. In the drawer, I found my mother's recent correspondence, bills, along with the detritus of modern life—paper clips, stamps, pens, and more. This was not so exciting.

However, once I opened the tambour doors, I discovered a captivating forgotten world of past lives, experiences, and emotions.

The first object I examined was a four-by-six-inch leather and silver commemorative *tabernacle individuel* that had celebrated my grandfather's first communion. It was printed with his initials, R. G. for René Gide (1891–1968), and dated May 31, 1903. Items like this are given as gifts to represent a personal altar or holy spot, perhaps a reminder that God is everywhere—not just within the walls of a full-sized church or temple. These tabernacles were inspired by the Jewish custom initiated by Moses, who provided a portable sanctuary for the Jewish tribes as they wandered on their journey to the Promised Land.

My grandfather's *tabernacle individuel* had working doors that opened like doors to a church. Inside, I found a warm engraving of Jesus, beaming, on a silver plate. Surrounded by cherubic angels, he offered bread and wine.

Next, I picked up a small, worn leather case, only a few inches wide but heavier than its size would indicate. Inside, I found the *Légion d'honneur* medallion my grandfather had received for his French military service during World War I. This item transported me. Established by Napoleon in 1802, the *Légion d'honneur* is the highest French order of merit for military and civil contribution. According to his service record, accessible online, Lieutenant René Gide received numerous citations for "unimaginable courage" and exemplary performance before being seriously injured on May 30, 1917, during the battle for the town of Craonne in northern France. During the First World War lieutenants, as a class of soldier, had the highest casualty rates in the armed forces. These were men who were expected to provide an example of bravery, unquestioned loyalty and commitment. They were the first in line leading the charge.

The town was destroyed. Interestingly, this area was also the site of a major battle that took place March 7, 1814, between

Napoleon's army and the combined forces of the Russian and Prussian armies.

Also in the desk were family photo albums of pictures from my mother's childhood. One amusing series showed my mother's family playing in the snow. My grandfather, formally dressed, looked stiff and cold. In characteristically French fashion, his *mégot* (cigarette butt) dangled dashingly. My grandmother wore elegant evening shoes and a full-length, stylish coat, complete with fur-lined collar and cuffs. She had a playful, menacing look on her face—snowball locked and loaded in her hands.

This was all that was left to me of my grandfather's life—mementos from his childhood, an award for his war service as a young man, and some photos of his role as husband and father. These fragments told many stories, yet they left more questions than answers. What had his childhood been like? How had he endured the horrors of war? Did he find joy in life? Unfortunately, I wouldn't find the answers in these items, and he had left few written words in response.

The secretary desk held one more treasure for me, one that would define the life and times of a different, older generation, a discovery that would not only afford insightful parallels to my lifetime but also encourage personal exploration.

Tucked inside the cabinet, I found an old book, as though it had been waiting there patiently for nearly a century. *La Vie qui passe*, published in 1922, now long out of print and forgotten, written by my great-grandfather, Félix Le Molt (1862–1923).

My mother—his granddaughter—had cherished this book. For her, it represented both family and France.

My mother was proud of her French family and heritage. Her house was filled with French books and cultural artifacts. She was a true French woman of intelligence, refinement, strength, and beauty. Her passion for France, its culture, and its language were ingrained and consistently impressed upon me. She embodied her country's love of intellectual ideas, skeptical individualism, abstract reasoning, and introspection. She was also contentious and a contrarian—recognizably challenging French traits. She instilled in my siblings and me a sense of history, an appreciation for art, and the comforting resilience of knowing and appreciating our cultural heritage. I am grateful for these gifts.

I was not unfamiliar with this book. My mother had insisted on using it during one of our Saturday morning sessions that she called *Les Leçons de Français*. During my childhood, as a supplement to my American grade school education, this weekly ordeal was an attempt to teach me how to speak, read, and write French. I resented it. I wanted nothing more than to go outside in the woods, rampaging with my pellet gun and my similarly weaponized band of brothers. I knew they were enjoying themselves while I suffered.

My mother desperately searched through *La Vie qui passe*, a book of 84 poems written over several decades in the early twentieth century, trying to find something—anything—that would appeal to the imagination of a young American boy. After several attempts to engage me with the seemingly arcane, abstruse French poems, she mercifully terminated her efforts, and I was released.

Although my mother never tried that again, she never stopped trying to impress upon us Humbert children the significance of her maternal grandfather's work. Twenty-five years after that failed attempt, she made copies of the book and distributed them to my siblings and me. None of us paid much attention to it. We had family and career concerns, and we had little interest in long-ago French poetry written by an unknown, long-deceased relative. We all promptly lost track of our copies. I did not lose track of my pellet gun, though. I still rampage through the woods with it and my band of brothers in my imagination.

Now I held in my possession the original book, published in France a century ago, and perhaps a copy that had even been handled by my great-grandfather. I was intrigued. Gingerly, I opened the old book. Many of the brown, roughly cut pages crumbled away from the spine. I spied several bookworms—*rats de bibliothèque* (equally repulsive in the French language)—busy at work. On the title page my mother, Annette, had written a statement.

To me. As though she had known I would find this.

Olivier, poésies écrits par ton arrière-grandpère maternel . . . A.

Olivier, Poems written by your maternal great-grandfather . . . *A.*

I could hear her voice as I read those words. This solitary sentence, simple and matter-of-fact, conveyed a responsibility but made no demands. I knew that my mother would have been thrilled to know that an effort had been made to have this book find its way into the lives of future generations. However, I also knew she would not want it viewed as an imposition.

The emotional heft of the legacy struck me: My mother had left me an original copy of her grandfather's book. My eyes welled up a bit, as I recalled her failed attempts to ignite my appreciation of this work, of which she was so proud. I may not have understood as a child, but I was now the keeper of this forgotten heirloom. It was up to me how—or if—I would (or could) pass on this legacy and its messages.

I certainly did not remember any of the poems from that dark *Leçon de Français* day, nor had I so much as opened the copy my mother had given me decades earlier. Now, as the assigned carrier of this story, I wanted to read the book. At first, I was confused—I couldn't find the table of contents.

Among the contrariness peculiar to the French is a publishing idiosyncrasy: the table of contents was hidden at the back of the book. Why the French insist on placing the table of contents at the back of the book is still a mystery to me.

Nonetheless, I began flipping pages from the back of the book. The first poem I encountered—the last poem of the book—was titled *Le vieux secrétaire,* "The Old Secretary Desk."

How strange. How appropriate.

In the reflective and melancholic poem, Félix Le Molt decries the fate of an old, abandoned desk, stored away 100 years ago, forlorn, neglected, and decaying. The desk Le Molt describes is a "tomb of memories," full of relics and links to forgotten worlds. He then juxtaposes this image with the death of an old friend whose body lies in her bedroom, where family and friends are paying their last respects. He describes her life as "an entire history run aground." This unnamed woman, too, carried memories of and connections to a past that would soon be forgotten. Time, as he warns, consumes memories like worms slowly devouring the desk. In the final stanza, he emphasizes the importance of carrying traditions and memories forward, no matter how small or insignificant they may seem, for the benefit of future generations. Although all living things eventually pass, this is how we keep the past, and our forebearers alive.

LE VIEUX SECRÉTAIRE (EXTRAIT)

Le vieux secrétaire ventru
De palissandre et bois de rose,
Dans le grenier, loin des intrus,
Depuis près d'un siècle repose.

Dans le secrétaire accueillant,
Nous rangeons nos pauvres reliques
Auprès des boîtes contenant
Bien des souvenirs identiques.
Ainsi se forgent les maillons
Dont est faite la forte chaîne
Guidant les générations
Au cours de leur route incertaine.

THE OLD SECRETARY DESK (EXCERPT)

The pot-bellied old secretary desk
Of palisander and rosewood,
In the attic, far from intruders, statuesque,
For almost a century, rests.

In the desk welcoming,
Our poor relics we keep
With nearby boxes containing
Similar souvenirs in heaps.
Thus are created the bonds
That forge a strong chain
Guiding our scions
Along their uncertain terrain.

I read the poem and then began to skim through others. I was surprised to find how much I enjoyed exercising my rusty French language skills. Even more, I felt the significance of reawakening my great-grandfather's voice and resurrecting his spirit. To my surprise, it didn't feel like a heavy weight of responsibility at all but rather an uplifting and deeply meaningful imperative. To study his words, feel his emotions, and relive his life moved me deeply. From his poems, I could see and feel what he saw and felt, and thus, he began to live again.

Félix Le Molt lived in a period in French history of unprecedented technological and societal changes that produced an era of nervous splendor. Characterized as a period of high artistic and cultural development, it also created the foundation for the modern world with all its dynamism and uncertainty. Life changing technological innovations were invented: electricity, elevators, aviation, motor vehicles, the telephone, and movies, to name a few. Society experienced the challenges of urbanization, a growing wealthy middle class and immigration. Major scientific discoveries were made in chemistry, physics, and exploration. Life became busier, more exciting, and faster-paced. This was *La Belle Époque*—the Beautiful Age.

By profession, Félix Le Molt had been a *juge d'instruction*, a judge of inquiry. His role was to conduct investigative hearings on serious criminal cases, collect facts, and determine if there was sufficient evidence to warrant a trial. In this book of poems, however, I began to understand that while he was dedicated to his profession, his passion was his poetry.

I had felt excited when I held my grandfather's *Légion d'honneur* medallion in my hands. I'd imagined the trials he faced, the ceremony held in his honor, and the pride and vindication he and his family must have felt. However, without his words, the experience felt incomplete.

By contrast, when I held my great-grandfather's book of poems and read his words, I experienced something quite different. He had opened a door and invited me to enter his thoughts and make his acquaintance.

I have always been interested in studying the physical artifacts and literature of prior civilizations. The idea of going back in history, appreciating different cultures, and seeing their world through their eyes fascinates me. A hauntingly beautiful visualization by the Buddhist monk Kendo Yoshida (1283–1350) elegantly captures my enchantment:

"To sit alone in the lamplight with a book spread out before you and hold intimate converse with men of unseen generations—such is a pleasure beyond compare."

This deteriorating book of long-forgotten poems, *La Vie qui passe*, felt like a recovered archeological artifact that offered insight into a lost world. This was not just any world but the world of one of my four great-grandfathers, and it was not just any artifact. I was holding in my hand the thoughts and feelings, the poetry, of Félix Le Molt.

How enticing to be able to discover and share in his life experiences.

My study of my great-grandfather's thoughts, life, and time accelerated during a troubling year, yet I found opportunities precisely because of those troubles. The first year of the COVID-19 pandemic and the social isolation it required created a favorable environment for reflection. Ironically, my great-grandfather, exactly one hundred years ago, had lived through a similar tragedy—the Spanish flu pandemic.

I had been given an invaluable gift: a rare opportunity to learn, think, and converse with an ancestor…and I had questions.

Bon-Papa

From his poetry, I knew that my great-grandfather would walk in the villages, fields, and forests around his family's country home in Bourbonne-les-Bains, using the experience to reinvigorate his mind and the place as a playground for his creativity. Then, in the evening, he contemplated and wrote poetry as a form of meditation and relaxation. I thought of how the English poet William Wordsworth explained this experience. According to him, poetry is "the spontaneous overflow of powerful feelings: it takes its origin from emotion recollected in tranquility."

My great-grandfather was introspective, self-aware, and emotionally supportive. Within his family, Félix Le Molt was affectionately known as *Bon-Papa* (good father). He was always spoken of as a man of integrity with high moral standards.

As I read Bon-Papa's poems, I saw that his poetic imagery, form, and style paint the portrait of a man uncomfortable with the pace of the social, economic, and political changes all around him. There was also personal and professional conflict. His poetry oscillates between the dark and the light, with an undercurrent of tension offset by calmness. The personal struggle to find balance is evident.

The following poems reflect this dichotomy:

"Nocturne" is bleak, fearful, and ghostly. An unnerving atmosphere of supernatural threat pervades the poem. Its latent malevolence feels like something Edgar Allen Poe would write.

NOCTURNE

La lune au teint blafard, au rire inquiétant,
Dans l'azur assombri, lentement se promène,
Se montre, disparaît et dessine en passant
Sur les prés endormis d'étranges phénomènes.

De ses rocs désolés, la mort et le néant
Trament leurs noirs complots contre la race humaine.
La lune au teint blafard, au rire inquiétant,
Dans l'azur assombri, lentement se promène.

Aussi malgré l'éclat discret de son croissant,
Bien que sa clarté soit enjôleuse et sereine,
L'âme du moribond et l'âme de l'enfant
Tressaillent, quand la nuit, complice, nous ramène
La lune au teint blafard, au rire inquiétant.

NOCTURNE

The pale moon with its laughter disquieting
In the clouded heavens, slowly wanders.
Shows itself, disappears, and creates in passing
On the sleeping meadows, strange wonders.

From its desolate rocks, death and nothing
Against humanity devise their dark maneuvers.
The pale moon with its laughter disquieting
In the clouded heavens, slowly wanders.

Despite the slender brightness of its crescent,
And though its clarity is calming and alluring,
The soul of the dying and the soul of the innocent
Shiver when the night, its accomplice, brings forth
The pale moon with its laughter disquieting.

Conversely, his poem "The Light in the Forest" is calming. This poem encapsulates the timeless inspirational themes of Nature's beauty and its ephemeral quality. There is a sense of serenity and security.

LA LUMIÈRE SOUS BOIS

La lumière est douce et sa face est sereine
Sous les bois on la voit s'avancer à pas lents;
Elle met un sourire à l'écorce du chêne,
Et la fougère mâle a des reflets d'argent.

Tout le long des sentiers, l'ombre en tremblant se traîne
Et par les chemins creux se faufile en rampant.
La lumière est douce et sa face est sereine
Sous les bois on la voit s'avancer à pas lents.

Dans les rais de soleil, fantasque et incertaine
La mouche aux ailes d'or s'élance en bourdonnant.
Apre sur les coteaux, cruelle dans la plaine,
Sous les halliers discrets aux tapis odorants
La lumière est douce et sa face est sereine.

THE LIGHT IN THE FOREST

The light is soft and its face serene,
Through the woods, we see its slow progression:
On the oak's bark, a smile beams,
The ferns show a silvery reflection.

Down the path, the trembling shadows careen
And by the sunken trails leave their impression.
The light is soft and its face serene,
Through the woods, we see its slow progression.

In the sun's rays, fanciful and wavering,
The fly with golden wings bombilates and plays.
Harsh on the hills, on the plains unrelenting,
But under hidden thickets, with fragrant baize,
The light is soft, and its face serene.

His poetry touched me and drew me into his world. I understood that his poems would have aided him in elucidating difficulties, appreciating the moment, and expressing himself. I wanted to learn more; I wanted to speak with him.

I love the French word *crépuscule*. Also available in English but rarely used, it means twilight. For me, the word conjures a magical, mystical time endowed with a unique light and sensitivity that intensifies colors and emotions. It is time suspended.

It was the perfect occasion to meet my great-grandfather, join him on his walk, and establish a personal connection.

"Good evening Bon-Papa, I would like you to know that I am translating your poems for your non-French-speaking descendants. I am grateful for the opportunity to become acquainted with you, your life and times, and to gain important lessons from your experiences. Thank you."

"Good evening Olivier! Non-French-speaking descendants! I cannot imagine that any of my ancestors would have thought such a thing possible. Please do not tell me they are German."

I laughed softly. "Don't worry, Bon-Papa, they are American."

"How interesting. Come walk with me, Olivier. Walking stimulates the mind, enhances the art of conversation, and draws out discoveries.

"America! What an enigma. Admired, feared, respected, and resented all at once. Clemenceau would surely not approve!"

I remembered that Georges ("The Tiger") Clemenceau had been Prime Minister of France during my great-grandfather's life. He was quoted as saying, "America is the only nation in history which, miraculously, has gone directly from barbarism to degeneration without the usual interval of civilization."

"In my day, many feared that America was a mechanized predator, bent on global domination, enslaving economies, cultures, and people. I read the works of Tocqueville, Lafayette, and Chateaubriand, and I chose to admire and respect the United States more than fear and criticize. And, of course, France must be grateful for America's support and sacrifices that broke the stalemate during the Great War, ending that horrific conflict."

"America was repaying the debt to France for its support during the American Revolution," I added.

"Indeed. During the celebration in Paris on July 4, 1917, America's Independence Day, a contingent of the American army marched to Lafayette's tomb. The American officer then proclaimed, 'Lafayette, we are here!'"

"The French soldier and aristocrat Marquis de Lafayette's assistance during the American Revolution was pivotal. America and France are very different culturally, but they have always been allies, and there is a strong connection, Bon-Papa."

These disparate cultural and philosophical views of America are an integral part of my identity, and they continue to be debated among the French. My parents respected both cultures but understood the difficulty in reconciling the two. They wanted their children to have, and to be, the best of both.

Bon-Papa continued reminiscing. "I was twenty-three when the Statue of Liberty was dedicated in the New York harbor."

This momentous copper statue—a gift from the French people commemorating the alliance between the two nations during the American Revolution—helped solidify the concept of "America" as a place of opportunity and potential, not only in the minds of the French, but in the minds of the entire world. It also, apparently, made a favorable impression on my great-grandfather.

Using flower seeds as a metaphor, Félix Le Molt promotes the concept of America as a place where the repressed, yet adventurous, can find new and exciting opportunities:

LES FLEURS DU TALUS (EXTRAIT)

Les plus fortes, les plus heureuses,
Trouvent le sol libérateur,
Ce talus des routes poudreuses
Qui est l'Amérique des fleurs.

THE FLOWERS OF THE EMBANKMENTS (EXCERPT)

The happiest, the strongest
Find liberated terrain,
In ridges and dusty roads they belong,
An America for flowers they attain.

"It was Gustave Eiffel who built the Statue of Liberty, and he then built the tower for *L'Exposition Universelle* (World's Fair) of 1889. *L'Exposition* was held to commemorate the 100-year anniversary of the French Revolution and was a unique opportunity for the world to see a new France. The event was a smashing success!

"Many nations from around the world participated and showcased their countries' culture. My nephew, Michel de Bellomayre, was fascinated with the United States. He was eight years old. I took him to the American exhibit.

"Michel was so excited to see the Buffalo Bill Wild West Show, which included a contingent of Sioux Indians and mock battles! He had read about the exploits of Buffalo Bill, and he was quite taken. He informed me that he and his young friends had made a pact. As soon as they were old enough, they would go live in the United States and have similar adventures!" (This incident is recorded in the personal unpublished diary—*Journal d'enfance*—of Michel Bellomayre, written from the ages of 6 to 14.)

"Bon-Papa, what a wonderful experience you had with the young, wide-eyed Michel! How exciting it must have been to see the city of Paris so transformed. How I wish I could have shared this significant historic event with you.

"What is best remembered about *L'Exposition Universelle* today is indeed Eiffel's tower, Bon-Papa. It is still standing, and has become the symbol of France."

"*Pas possible!*" exclaimed my great-grandfather. "That monstrosity! It looks like a factory chimney. First you tell me I have descendants who do not speak French, and now I am to learn that Eiffel's tower was never removed!"

At the time, Eiffel's tower was met with great ambivalence by much of the French population. In some segments, it was viewed with overt hostility. *La Tour d'Eiffel* was a new concept: It wasn't Greek, nor Gothic, nor Renaissance. It was modern and, for some, disconcerting. Of course, that was the whole point. It was the perfect representative of the potential of the modern age. It heralded society's progress, along with growing beliefs in science and technology, while creating a unique work of art that endures today.

"Bon-Papa, I am so sorry for upsetting you."

"Don't worry, Olivier. It's not serious. I did warn that releasing my poems could be unsettling. My poems are like poisonous mushrooms!"

Poisonous Mushrooms

"Bon-Papa, in your poem 'Préface' you do actually compare your poems to poisonous mushrooms that have grown quietly in the shadows without drawing attention to themselves. You state that they are unimportant and better left alone. You further, then, imply that there could be potentially dangerous consequences in exposing them to a wider audience. What a clever way to create temptation and interest!"

PRÉFACE

Comme des champignons quelque peu vénéneux,
Ces rondeaux ont poussé sous bois, dans la fougère,
Dans la calme forêt, aux bruits mystérieux,
Où le bonheur est grand et la peine légère.

Parfois, on les lisait le soir, à la lumière,
Et puis, le lendemain, on ne parlait plus d'eux.
Comme des champignons quelque peu vénéneux,
Ces rondeaux ont poussé sous bois, dans la fougère.

Pourquoi vont-ils sortir de leur sommeil heureux?
Mieux valait un tiroir pour demeure dernière.
Ils n'ont rien à gagner d'un jour trop lumineux;
Je crains que leur lecture, hélas! ne se digère
Comme des champignons quelque peu vénéneux.

Rouen, 1922

PREFACE

Like mushrooms that are somewhat poisonous,
These verses grew among ferns, under wood,
In the calm forest with noises mysterious,
Where trouble is gentle, and there is much good.

Sometimes, they were read by lamp light luminous,
And then next morning forgotten for good,
Like mushrooms that are somewhat poisonous,
These verses grew among ferns, under wood.

Why should they awaken from their happy night?
In the back of a drawer, it is better to stay.
They have nothing to gain from the sunlight;
That their message not be digested, I pray,
Like mushrooms somewhat poisonous.

Rouen, 1922

My great-grandfather smiled. "The ancient Egyptians put curses, warnings in the Pharaohs' tombs to frighten people away, 'as for all men who shall enter this my tomb... impure... there will be judgment ... an end shall be made for him.' Most dissuading, don't you think? But, of course, it did just the opposite.

"Seriously, I did believe that some people would be offended by some of the poems' messages and, in turn, face painful self-reflection. Readers may confront difficult (poisonous) truths about themselves and their perceptions of the world."

"Bon-Papa, you provide some insight as to who might be offended with the insertion of the words *'quelque peu.'* The poems are 'somewhat' poisonous. Is their perilousness dependent upon the reader's level of 'purity' or 'impurity' and how the reader thus interprets each poem?"

"Olivier, reflection requires courage. It is a thoughtful and deliberate process that we all struggle with, if we choose to do it. Societal and familial constraints, economic realities, and educational, religious, and political indoctrinations all conspire to shape our perceptions of who we are and what we believe in. We become what is expected of us. How difficult it is to accept truths that run counter to what we have been led to believe.

"But we can make conscious choices to guide us in how best to live. The Roman orator and statesman Cicero tells us, 'It is not by muscle, speed, or physical dexterity that great things are achieved, but by reflection, force of character, and judgment.'"

"A man with just those qualities wrote an incisive introduction to your book of poems, Bon-Papa."

Mauriac

The introduction to *La Vie qui passe* was written by François Mauriac. I confess to having known nothing about him. I subsequently learned that he was one of the French literary greats of the twentieth century. François Mauriac (1885–1970) would become a recipient of the Grand Cross of the French *Légion d'honneur* and a member of the *Académie française*. These were not his greatest accomplishments. In 1952, he received the Nobel Prize in Literature for "the deep spiritual insight and the artistic intensity with which he has in his novels penetrated the drama of human life."

Mauriac was known for his beautiful economy of words and psychological insight, and, true to form, his introduction to *La Vie qui passe* brilliantly and succinctly reveals the essence of Félix Le Molt:

Monsieur,

J'ai beaucoup aimé ce recueil dont m'a séduit surtout le ton modéré et discret; aucune emphase, bien que, malgré cette bonhomie, on sente, à plus d'un vers, que le poète serait capable de planer; mais il préfère s'en tenir à une musique très simple. Les «moralités» de certains rondeaux, l'intention didactique de plusieurs, rattachent ce livre à la meilleure, à la plus saine tradition. Evidemment sa forme, à quelques-uns paraîtra surannée. Pour moi j'en apprécie la sagesse bourgeoise. Dans la vieille France, les magistrats se délassaient souvent à traduire Horace; celui-ci fait mieux: il note, il fixe ses impressions quotidiennes. Il ne fait point fi de la vie. Il se promène dans un jardin modeste où tout le charme. Il ne s'y attache pas trop, sachant qu'il le faudra quitter un jour et il sourit comme Candide.

Je vous prie, Monsieur, de me croire votre admirateur,

FRANÇOIS MAURIAC

Sir,

I very much enjoyed this collection, which seduced me with its discreet and moderate tone. There is none of the grandiosity that, despite the poet's playfulness, one senses in more than one verse that he would be capable of soaring into. He prefers to content himself with very simple music. The "moralities" of certain rondeaux, with didactic intent in some, connect this book with a sounder tradition. Certainly, this style, in several of the poems, appears old-fashioned. But, as for me, I appreciate its bourgeois wisdom. In old France, the magistrates often enjoyed translating Horace; this poet does it better: he observes and notes his daily impressions. He is not detached from life. He strolls in a modest garden where everything delights him. He does not allow himself to become too attached, knowing that one day he will have to leave, and he smiles like Candide.

I request, Sir, that you believe me to be your admirer,

FRANÇOIS MAURIAC

Le Molt was 60—nearly twice Mauriac's age—when he published *La Vie qui passe*. To have the younger, emerging luminary read his book of poems and contribute a letter of acclamation was quite an honor. How did such a renowned literary giant as Mauriac come to know and appreciate Félix Le Molt and his poetry? The relationship seems incongruous, given their vast differences in age, profession, and social circumstances. I needed to find out.

I recognized some of the furniture. I could have been in my mother's house, but Bon-Papa and I were sitting comfortably in the living room at Bourbonne-les-Bains. The musical instruments—piano, harp, cello—felt familiar, as did the artwork and ambiance. We were having an afternoon *tisane* or herbal tea.

"Bon-Papa, having an introduction written by François Mauriac was quite a coup. How did that happen?"

"My daughter, your grandmother Antoinette, married René Gide. René's first cousin, Paul Sarrut, was friends with François Mauriac. Your grandparents enjoyed an extensive literary social circle that also included André Maurois, another good friend of Mauriac. They arranged an introduction for me."

"I have seen pictures of my grandmother at a reception with André Maurois. How fortunate to have such literary connections!"

"Yes, such wonderful people, such powerful minds."

"I read that Mauriac had his first critical success, *Le Baiser au lépreux* (*The Kiss for the Leper*), in 1922—the same year your book of poems *La Vie qui passe* was published."

"Yes, but *The Kiss for the Leper* was considered scandalous upon publication because it dealt openly with sexual feelings and desires. Unfortunately, my little book of poems did not enjoy such notoriety!"

I enjoyed his playfulness. "Tell me of your conversations with M. Mauriac, Bon-Papa."

"I invited him into my library, and I congratulated him on his new book. He acknowledged that it had created controversy. I remember his concern that the Church would not be happy with him."

A practicing Catholic, Mauriac nonetheless wrote unflinchingly about religious repression and hypocrisy, as well as the conflict between human passion and religious virtue. He was appalled by the Catholic Church's indifference to injustice and the way it condoned anti-Semitism.

"Did he ask you what your favorite books were?" I asked excitedly.

"He asked that question a bit differently in an interestingly thought-provoking way. He stated that he could tell who I was by knowing what I read, but wanting to know me better and know what was in my heart, he asked me what I reread. I told him that I frequently returned to the wisdom of the ancients."

"The ancients? What do you mean by that, Bon-Papa?"

"I am referring to the Greco-Roman philosophers. Their compelling cultural, intellectual, and literary ideas can guide us."

I had noticed that *La Vie qui passe* was replete with references to Greek and Roman gods such as Venus, Parca, Janus, Pan, and Apollo. My great-grandfather was obviously well versed in the culture and mythology of classical antiquity.

"Bon-Papa, in your poem 'The Marble Vase' you allude to the 'secret soul of the ancients'. Your appreciation for their intellectualism and sensuality is on full display!"

LE VASE DE MARBRE

Les nymphes des bosquets, en blanches théories
Dansent pour le plaisir des héros et des dieux;
Et c'est en contemplant ces pâles effigies
Qu'on trouve le secret de l'âme des aïeux
Qui entouraient l'amour, la jeunesse, la vie,
La femme et la beauté de mille soins pieux.
Les nymphes des bosquets, en blanches théories
Dansent pour le plaisir des héros et des dieux.

Les satyres barbus, lorgnent avec envie
Sur les anses, juchés, le cortège joyeux;
Leur face où sont unis le vice et l'ironie
Donne encor plus d'attraits aux corps voluptueux
Souples et alignés en blanche théories.

THE MARBLE VASE

The nymphs of the gardens, dressed in ivory
For the pleasure of heroes and gods, dance merrily,
And in contemplating these pale effigies,
The secret soul of the ancients is revealed artfully.
They embrace love, life, vitality,
Women, beauty, and a thousand precious qualities.
The nymphs of the gardens, dressed in ivory
For the pleasure of heroes and gods, dance merrily.

The bearded satyrs leer with envy
On the handles, they watch the joyous harmony;
Their faces display both vice and irony
Accentuating the voluptuous bodies,
Supple and well-formed, dressed in ivory.

"Olivier, these philosophies can help us achieve what the ancients called *arete*—our full potential in moral excellence and character. They can guide us in pursuing what is most valuable so that we are not in danger of wasting our lives."

"Some of your poems contain moral lessons or "moralities" as Mauriac notes. Was your purpose instructive?"

"Yes, I wanted to encourage my readers to adopt basic moral principles, engage in self-reflection, examine their values, and develop an appreciation for what makes us human.

"To avoid sounding too pretentious, I used the French medieval rondeau format, which has songlike qualities. I wanted to both instruct and delight.

"Nevertheless, M. Mauriac thought me 'old fashioned!'"

Bon-Papa sat pouting with a deceptively affected despondency. The smile in his eyes gave him away. I comfortingly poured him more tea.

"M. Mauriac said he admired your wisdom, Bon-Papa. I did enjoy his depiction of you: 'He strolls in a modest garden where everything delights him.' Many of your poems are meditations on the natural world, plants, animals, the countryside, and the cycle of life."

Bon-Papa bounced back. "Nature is a teacher and does not deceive. We should live in accordance with nature. Nature presents opposites, yet these contrasts are actually complementary. There is continuous change, yet also balance and harmony. These forces do not detract or minimize but enhance each other."

The poem "Mirage" is an example of Félix Le Molt's use of the natural world to introduce a morality.

MIRAGE

Ombrageant l'eau qui dort, de vieux arbres, géants
Immuables et droits se dressent vers les nues;
Leurs fûts, vêtus de gui méprisent l'ouragan;
Seul, on voit, près des nids, la feuille qui remue.

Quand ils vont se mirer, ces arbres, dans l'étang
Leurs troncs ne forment plus que lignes saugrenues.
Tout le long du canal, de vieux arbres, géants
Immuables et droits se dressent vers les nues.

C'est par ses propres yeux qu'on doit juger les gens:
Le reflet de la glace augmente ou atténue;
Tout miroir est doué d'un pouvoir déformant
Ne nous laissons pas prendre à la ligne imprévue
Qui présentent dans l'eau les vieux arbres géants.

Versailles

MIRAGE

The old giant trees shading the sleeping water,
Immutable and upright, reach up toward the skies,
Their trunks, draped in mistletoe, despise the thunder;
Near the birds' nests, a leaf's movement catches our eye.

The reflection of these trees in the pond
Reveal their trunks in ludicrous guise.
The old giant trees along the canal becalmed,
Immutable and upright, reach up toward the skies.

Only from one's own eyes can we judge the other.
The reflection of the glass may deflate or augment.
All mirrors are gifted with the ability to alter.
Let us not take the incorrect sentiment
That the old giant trees reflect on the water.

Versailles

"Your concerns and the advice imparted through your poem 'Mirage' to combat prejudice are laudable. You warn us to beware of the powerful forces that exist within our society and ourselves that can alter and distort our perceptions of others.

"I see why Mauriac refers to the Roman poet Horace in his introduction to your book of poems. Like Horace, you are a thoughtful, reflective observer who uses lyrical poetry to draw attention to disconcerting social attitudes and injustice. Your poems teach fundamental truths, Bon-Papa."

"It is a comparison I do not deserve, Olivier, but thank you.

"Poetry has the potential to make us feel, and look beyond ourselves and see another world, but we must take the time, slow down, and ask questions. Plato said, '"The right question is usually more important than the right answer."'

"The question you raise in your poem 'The Song of the Waterdrops' is challenging Bon-Papa. Why are there differences in things despite their seemingly identical natures?"

LE CHANT DES GOUTTES D'EAU

Chaque goutte qui tombe a un son différent
Et donne à sa chanson sa note personnelle.
Le chant des gouttes d'eau, narquois et sautillant
Semble parfois l'écho de quelque villanelle.

Au fond du vase obscur on dirait qu'on entend
D'un violon lointain vibrer la chanterelle.
Chaque goutte qui tombe a un son différent
Et donne à sa chanson sa note personnelle.

Parfois sa voix est grave, austère, solennelle,
Puis brusquement éclate en un rire d'enfant,
Le mystère insondé, c'est que rien ne décèle

Pourquoi du même endroit au même point chutant
Chaque goutte qui tombe a un son différent.

THE SONG OF WATERDROPS

Each drop that falls has a different harmony
And gives the song its personal artistry.
The drops of water mocking, hopping musically,
Resemble at times the echo of poetry.

At the bottom of the vase we hear obscurely
A distant violin's vibrating melody.
Each drop that falls has a different harmony
And gives the song its personal artistry.

At times, its voice is serious, solemn, surly,
Then abruptly bursts in childish laughter and shouts.
It cannot be resolved, an unsolved mystery,
Why from the same spot, the same spout
Each drop that falls has a different harmony.

"It is that sense of wonder that inspires and transforms us. According to Socrates, without wonder, Olivier, there is no wisdom. Can we appreciate the duality around us? Are we threatened or enchanted, or do we even notice?"

While M. Mauriac was impressed with the quality of my great-grandfather's poetry, he was more interested in how it expressed the qualities of Félix Le Molt.

The last sentence in Mauriac's introduction—"He does not allow himself to become too attached, knowing that one day he will have to leave, and he smiles like Candide"—moved me profoundly and left me perplexed. Both emotions washed over me, first with Mauriac's message of transience and gentle sadness, then with its unexpected reference to *Candide*.

Candide's Smile

I was familiar with Voltaire's book *Candide: or, The Optimist* (1759). Indeed, I would count Voltaire, a poet and renowned philosopher, as one of my historical heroes. A true genius of the Enlightenment, he represented its many facets and magnificence with brilliant intellectual, humorous, and human insights. Having Voltaire as a dinner companion would have been an enthralling occurrence.

Mauriac's comparison of Candide to my great-grandfather subtly provided some discerning information about Félix Le Molt.

Candide is a powerful satirical refutation of the then-prevailing philosophical idea that because the world was created by God and God is supernal, then the world we live in must be the best world possible. What humans perceive as evil, therefore, is just their ignorance of the higher forces working to enhance the greater good.

This worldview was championed by the German polymath Gottfried Wilhelm Leibniz, as well as the Catholic Church. By extension, then, it was the worldview of most French citizens of the time. It appealed, however simplistically, to both religious dogma and societal custom. By accepting God's supremacy over everything in the human world, humans didn't have to trouble themselves with concerns like injustice, genocide, poverty, hunger, and the like.

Voltaire was a man of the Enlightenment (1685–1815), a period of scientific, religious, and cultural evolution. As an artist and philosopher, he questioned traditional views. Voltaire excoriated intellectual laziness and dishonesty; consequently he championed that the application of reason should supersede the reliance on revelation—an unpopular view with the more conservative and religious factions of society.

Voltaire was deeply affected by the Great Lisbon Earthquake of 1755, which killed approximately 50,000 people. He found it unconscionable that State and Church officials rationalized this tragic event as simply "God's will" and "for the best."

He wanted societies to use the power of reason and science to understand such events. This would allow them to better prepare for future tragedies and mitigate the damage. In Voltaire's view, it was irresponsible and immoral to create answers based on blind faith or naïve optimism. Especially abhorrent was the prevailing belief that such cataclysmic events were the result of divine retribution. Still today, in some segments of society, there exists an undercurrent of acceptance that natural disasters are a deserved punishment for iniquity. After hurricanes, floods, earthquakes, and even solar eclipses religious fundamentalists and unethical political leaders can always be found who are quick to proclaim that these events are manifestations of God's wrath on an impious people.

The title character in *Candide* is an innocent, sheltered young man who has been raised to believe that everything that happens is God's will and, therefore, for the best. When he is cast out into the world, however, he must confront the world's harshest realities, its pain and suffering. Readers witness Candide's painful disillusionment and his realization that life is more complicated than he was taught to believe.

Candide endures numerous trials and achieves relative success despite his disillusionment. The novel concludes with Candide's practical response when he is questioned about life's vicissitudes:

> *"Cela est bien dit, répondit Candide, mais il faut cultiver notre jardin."*
>
> "All that is very well," answered Candide, "but let us cultivate our garden."

From all his travels, adventures, and tribulations, Candide learns that we stand a better chance of finding happiness if we first focus on our immediate environment, find productive work, and care for those around us. Rather than acquiescing to the world's strife as simply "God's will," Voltaire, through Candide, suggests responding in a local, realistic, and practical way.

By the novel's conclusion, Candide has made peace with himself and the world around him. He is neither detached from nor unduly attached to the flow of events. This perspective offers him equanimity and inner calm.

In the introduction to *La Vie qui passe*, François Mauriac concludes that Félix Le Molt had achieved this rare inner state. My great-grandfather understood that to appreciate life more, we must let go of our egos and desires/attachments.

Many of Félix Le Molt's poems demonstrate a philosophical acceptance of our ephemeral passage through time. "The Dying Candle" uses scent and sound to illuminate Le Molt's thoughts about the tenuous and fleeting nature of human life.

LE CIERGE QUI S'ÉTEINT

Du cierge mourant, la tremblante fumée
Mêle son âcre odeur aux notes du plain-chant;
Et puis, on n'entend plus, dans l'église fermée,
Que des vieux bois meurtris les longs gémissements.

Les senteurs que répand la mêche consumée
Evoquent dans nos cœurs mille tableaux poignants.
Du cierge mourant, la tremblante fumée
Mêle son âcre odeur aux notes du plain-chant.

Du baptême à la mort, la vie est résumée
Dans ce fade parfum vers les voûtes montant;
Quand on songe aux relais dont la vie est semée,
On trouve au souvenir triste ou gai se mêlant,
Du cierge jauni la tremblante fumée.

THE DYING CANDLE

From the dying candle, the trembling smoke
Mixes its acrid odor with the plainchant singing:

Then, from the closed church no further note,
Except the creaking of the old wood, groaning.

From the aromas of the spent wick, the scent evokes
In our hearts, a thousand thoughts overwhelming.
From the dying candle, the trembling smoke
Mixes its acrid odor with the plainchant singing.

From baptism to death, life is condensed
In this bland fragrance rising to the ceiling.
Reflecting on life's connections and significance,
We find a mixture of sad and happy feelings,
From the yellowed candle and its trembling smoke.

There is a Japanese term (*mono no aware,* an empathy toward things) for the emotion Le Molt describes. It is a quietly elated, bittersweet feeling of being profoundly part of the transient, awe-inspiring wonders of life, made more poignant by the knowledge that all is simply borrowed and must ultimately be given back. That realization makes life all the more significant, accepting transience to live more fully.

"…and he smiles like Candide."

La Vie Qui Passe

When my mother left me a first edition of her grandfather's poetry book, I took it as an assignment to pass along his legacy to his descendants and anyone else who might be interested. I would need to translate these poems and supply some societal and historical context.

My translations have little literary value in comparison to my great-grandfather's original French poems. I simply intended to convey the literal sense of the lines while attempting to maintain some poetic spirit. I translated them following his original poetic form and rhyme scheme, and I strove not to sacrifice reason for rhyme.

The poems in *La Vie qui passe* are a real-time anthology of Le Molt's thoughts and emotions. They offer a portal through time for us to explore his era and personal thoughts. They express the sentiments of a private and seemingly solitary man. Le Molt recorded what he saw, smelled, heard, felt, and dreamt. Through his senses, he unleashed his curiosity and imagination and was able to fully explore the experience creatively. Yet, he still left room for response, even a century or more later.

"Bon-Papa, M. G. Dubose, writing in the *Journal de Rouen,* gave your book of poems a glowing review."

Here is an ensemble of delicate impressions, of intimate and subtle scenes beautifully evoked by a writer whose refined morality, optimism, and goodness have withstood the daily sight of all vices, baseness, and infamy that paraded themselves before his court. He presents it all in his poems, discreet and harmonious, with nuances and variations of hue and thought, bringing ingenuity while staying true to poetic form. As Mr. François Mauriac so rightly puts it in his preface, the poet in Mr. Félix Le Molt comes out of the soundest French literary tradition.

"Well, unlike M. Mauriac, I am not sure he understood me or my poems. We must also judge compliments. After all, I was an influential member of the Rouen judiciary. As such, hidden agendas and ulterior motives are always a concern. However, it is generally better to be praised by someone else than by yourself."

"It is a daunting prospect to translate poems that 'come out of the soundest French literary tradition.' I am concerned I will not do you justice, Bon-Papa."

"You are doing a good thing. I am honored that you are releasing my voice into another language. We never know whether the little things we do in the present will be gathered by those in the future and transformed into something bigger.

"How much smaller our worlds would be without translations! Imagine how limited our minds and spirits would be if we were limited to poetry and literature written in our native tongues. One could argue that translations are unique works unto themselves, ones that both reflect and build upon the original works.

"But you will need to make a choice, Olivier. Translated poems are like lovers. The unattractive are faithful while the beautiful ones are unfaithful. Rarely can you have both!"

His analogy made me smile. "I fear my translations will not be beautiful, but I hope they are faithful. Bon-Papa, help me understand the title of your book, *La Vie qui passe*. This is a most difficult phrase. It does not translate well into English but speaks so profoundly and distinctly in the French language."

"Indeed, it is an expression more felt than explainable."

"This expression for me, Bon-Papa, evokes the concept of time flowing beyond our control, slipping through our fingers. It feels melancholic."

"Yes, it does, but I will quote the great philosopher Michel de Montaigne, France's national sage, to give you my sense: 'I do not portray the thing in itself. I portray the passage from day to day, from minute to minute.' Rather than projecting a sense of helplessness or loss, I wanted to stress the importance of being aware of life's incremental passage and the evolution of our thoughts and emotions. Time is not passing; rather, we are flowing through it."

We walked in silence for a few moments. "So, Bon-Papa, your objective was to bear witness and pay tribute to life's journey without being elegiac. Your message is less about life slipping away and more about the journey's potential."

"Yes. We have a tendency to decry or deny our passage through time and its effects. We seek to evade the inevitability of change. Olivier, we must remember and accept that everything constantly moves and changes. I struggled with this reality throughout my life."

"Heraclitus tells us, 'You can never step into the same river twice,'" I ventured, attempting to contribute to the conversation.

"Such appropriate imagery! I eventually discovered that time is not linear or circular; it simply allows for the flow of change. I also choose to recognize that each present moment—a culmination of moments immeasurable—can be immortalized. I want to find eternity in my daily impressions.

"For example, in my poem 'The Pale Light of the Crocus,' I focus on the moment and am awed by the complexities of Nature, its eternal, evolving essence, and the mysteries of its duality."

LA PÂLE LUMIÈRE DU COLCHIQUE

Sur les prés le colchique allume sa veilleuse
Alors que le soleil s'éteint à l'horizon;
Etrange feu follet sur l'écharpe onduleuse
De la nuit, qui s'en vient surprendre les gazons.

Messager annonçant la saison rigoureuse,
Frêle enfant de l'automne à la fauve toison,
Sur les prés le colchique allume sa veilleuse
Alors que le soleil s'éteint à l'horizon.

Sous le voile trompeur d'une grâce charmeuse,
Sa mortelle beauté enfante le poison;
Le soir, pour embellir sa tige vénéneuse,
Portant avec orgueil de mauves floraisons,
Sur les prés le colchique allume sa veilleuse.

Bourbonne

THE PALE LIGHT OF THE CROCUS

In the meadow the crocuses alight
While the sun descends on its ambit voyage;
On rolling hills strange will-o'-wisps in sight
Startling the grasses and tillage.

Heralding the upcoming season's plight,
Autumn's frail child of saffron pelage,
In the meadow the crocuses alight
While the sun descends on its ambit voyage.

With false premise and abundant charm,
Within her fateful beauty, toxicity abides;
At night, to embellish its stem of harm,
Violet flowers displayed with pride,
In the meadow the crocuses alight.

Bourbonne

Le Molt's poems create dramatic moments within everyday occurrences, and they illustrate the evocative power of well-crafted sensory images. His poetry encourages readers to slow down and appreciate their surroundings and the infinite possibilities therein. His poems have a haiku-like quality with their deceptive brevity, firm adherence to form, seasonal allusions, and distinct shifts in the last stanzas. Each one shares a similar intensity.

However, despite Bon-Papa's illumination, I still could not determine an appropriate translation for *La Vie qui passe*. Like his poems, the expression is pensive, pithy, and wonderfully graceful. Any attempt sounded banal: "as time goes by," "life as it passes," and "life going by" are all wrong, so I changed the subject.

"Bon-Papa, why did you start writing poetry?"

"Olivier, did you know the word 'poetry' is of Greek origin and stems from a Greek verb meaning 'to create'? Rodin's sculpture *The Thinker* was initially named *The Poet*. Rodin's intention was to represent a poet who was determined to use the power of thought to create. Rodin instinctively understood the importance of contemplation; he had the extraordinary capacity to portray the human spirit within his art.

"He aroused us all with his exhortation, 'The main thing is to be moved, to love, to tremble, to live!' Such powerful and positive words. I wrote poetry for *exactly* these reasons. I wanted to tremble, not out of fear but from an appreciation of life and the excitement derived from the creative process.

"Experiences shape who we are, Olivier. The experience of writing poetry made me more thoughtful, more humane."

"But Bon-Papa, many of your poems are melancholic. Were you happy?"

Happiness

"Olivier, have you heard the expression 'Melancholy is the happiness of being sad'? It was written by Victor Hugo. This is another one of those phrases that is either intrinsically understood or becomes inexplicable."

I had not heard this expression, but I understood and appreciated its subtle insight.

"Melancholy is a complex emotion often confused, or mistakenly associated, with sorrow. Unlike the hopelessness and despair that sorrow brings, melancholy is a state of pensive reflection, an acknowledgment of raw emotions in a yearning to experience them more deeply. The process can make one feel more alive by providing inspiration to appreciate the here and now and by recognizing how fleeting the present is."

"I feel that when I see a sunset. I am not sad, but tears come to my eyes. Your poem 'The Old Garden' evokes that feeling. The poem reveals the tender longing and bittersweet joy you find through your observations and feelings."

LE VIEUX JARDIN

Rien ne vaut la douceur triste du vieux jardin
Qui végète, assoupi dans sa mélancolie
Et qui semblè écouter quelque clocher lointain
Contant les souvenirs d'une époque abolie.

Auprès du fier soleil, du phlox dur et hautain
Tremble la clématite en sa grâce amollie.
Rien ne vaut la douceur triste du vieux jardin
Qui végète, assoupi dans sa mélancolie.

Entre les buis taillés, c'est là, frêle et jolie
Que la belle-de-nuit regarde avec dédain
La nigelle aux yeux bleus; que la tendre ancolie
Dans ses urnes reçoit les larmes du matin…
Rien ne vaut la douceur triste du vieux jardin!
Pour Ph.

Bourbonne-les-Bains, Juin 1913

THE OLD GARDEN

Nothing compares to the sad sweetness of the old garden
Which vegetates, dozing in its melancholy,
To a distant bell it seems to hearken
Reawakening memories of a bygone history.

Facing the proud sun, next to phlox, haughty and hardened,
Trembles the clematis, with softened beauty.
Nothing compares to the sad sweetness of the old garden
Which vegetates dozing in its melancholy.

Between the carved boxwood, there, fragile and lovely,
The marvel of Peru looks scorning

At the blue-eyed nigella; that the columbine dainty
In its urns receives the tears of the morning…
Nothing compares to the sad sweetness of the old garden!
For Ph.
Bourbonne-les-Bains, June 1913

"Olivier, melancholy is a shroud I enjoy wrapping myself in. I find it somehow comforting. Perhaps I indulge a bit too much. We must avoid creating a melancholic state as a permanent condition. The melancholy in my poems are meditative exercises that gave me guidance, perspective, and equilibrium."

"Autumn is a recurring theme in many of your poems, Bon-Papa. What was it about autumn that you found so compelling?"

"It represents the transient nature of life. We sense a leaving behind of a part of us, yet it is such a celebration of all the senses. Nature appears to be dying, but presents us with a spectacular final burst of life. It is this beginning of a great change that combines energy and entropy which accentuates the season's beauty. We feel this momentum with senses rendered more perceptive.

"And as Gustave Flaubert put it, 'It is the season that suits memories so well!'"

L'AUTOMNE

Voilà l'automne qui s'avance
Semant de l'or sur les coteaux;
Il a le calme et l'opulence
Des trois mages orientaux

Qui suivaient l'étoile en silence
Pour voir Jésus dans son berceau…
Voilà l'automne qui s'avance
Semant de l'or sur les coteaux.

La caille a fui vers la Provence
La vieille, au bois, fait des fagots,
Sur l'aire sèche la semence,
Le berger rentre son troupeau,
Voilà l'automne qui s'avance! …

Bourbonne, 1913

AUTUMN

Autumn makes its entrance
Sowing gold on the hill's gradient.
He has the calm and opulence
Of the three kings of the Orient
Who followed the star in silence
To see Jesus in his cradle, radiant.
Autumn makes its entrance
Sowing gold on the hill's gradient.

The quail, toward Provence have flown,
The old woman makes her wooden stacks,
The seeds dry air-blown.
The shepherd returns with his pack.
Autumn makes its entrance! …

Bourbonne, 1913

I enjoy walking through the woods on crisp and clear New England autumn evenings with my great-grandfather's poetic spirit, reflecting on life's passages. I hear the distinctive sound of my feet shuffling through dead leaves and the mournful honking farewell of migrating Canada geese flying south. I feel the soft coolness of the air on my cheeks and taste its sweetness. I smell earth and smoke. I am awed by the sight of magnificent colors by day and the vibrant sunset, as its rays give a final radiant kiss to downy clouds. A reassuring serenity descends. This beauty, and a reflective melancholy, are some of autumn's gifts.

Félix Le Molt, as François Mauriac notes in his introduction, is neither detached from nor too attached to the world around him. He accepts the transient nature of life and consciously observes and lives with sensitivity. The following poem uses the transitionary nature of autumn to encourage us not to dwell on the past:

L'ODEUR DES BOIS, EN AUTOMNE (EXTRAIT)

Des souvenirs fanés, hélas! Que nous importe
De voir s'éterniser la grisante douceur!...
Pour que le vent d'automne avec lui les emporte,
Par son souffle mêlant la peine et le bonheur,
Du passé, nous aussi, grattons la feuille morte.

THE SCENT OF THE WOODS IN AUTUMN (EXCERPT)

Faded memories, alas! It matters futilely
How long endures their intoxicating tenderness! ...
Allow the winds of autumn to take them freely,
With a gust, combine pain and happiness,
Regarding the past, we too kick up dead leaves.

"I will answer your question. Yes, I was happy, but I had to learn to be happy. I drew inspiration from Paul Valéry's poem 'The Graveyard by the Sea.' In the poem, the poet has the weight of the past, the tombstones, at his back, and the infinite sea and horizon in front of him. In this liminal space, he contemplates life and death, love and loss, the relentless passage of life, and concludes that he cannot remain indecisive, stagnant, and unhappy and that he must make a choice. He chooses to move forward rather than dwell on the past: *Le vent se lève…il faut tenter de vivre!* ('The wind rises… we must try to live!'). Discarding the damaging anchors of the past, he seeks to acquire a calm confidence in the future."

Félix Le Molt's poem "*La pépite d'or*" ("The Golden Nugget") offers us this meditation:

LA PEPITE D'OR

L'humble pépite d'or chemine au fond des eaux
Parant d'un fauve éclat les limons et les sables:
Dans son isolement, ce n'est qu'un grain plus beau
Prïs dans le tourbillon d'autres grains innombrables.

Que d'efforts, que de soins pour en faire un lingot,
Pour former un joyau de sa poudre impalpable!
L'humble pépite d'or chemine au fond des eaux
Parant d'un fauve éclat les limons et les sables.

Notre bonheur, non plus, quoi qu'en pensent les sots,
N'est pas un plat qu'un jour on trouve sur la table;

Heureux qui sait grouper, choisir, mettre en faisceau
Ses éléments impondérables,
Humbles pépites d'or cheminant sous les eaux!
Paris.

THE GOLDEN NUGGET

The humble gold nugget shuffles downstream
Adorning silt and sand with fawn-colored radiance;
In its isolation, it is simply a grain that gleams
Caught in the whirlwind with grains miscellaneous.

Such effort and care, to make an ingot beam,
To form a jewel from its powder's brilliance!
The humble gold nugget shuffles downstream
Adorning silt and sand with fawn-colored radiance.

Our happiness, no less, whatever fools deem
Is not a plate we simply find on our table;
Happy are those who know how to sort and seam
Its elements imponderable,
The humble gold nugget shuffles downstream!
Paris.

"The Golden Nugget" shows us that even though we are "caught in the whirlwind" the resourcefulness gained from the rough and tumble of life's journey, combined with the deliberate, thoughtful application of good judgment, provides us the potential to emerge resplendent.

Félix Le Molt concluded that our happiness requires conscious effort and that it does not happen by itself. Perhaps some of us have to work a little harder to achieve it. My great-grandfather further understood the supportive role family plays in enabling us to "sort and seam" life's challenges and mysteries.

Family

La *Vie qui passe* is dedicated to my great-grandfather's wife, Marie. It is a lovely and poetic tribute and, of course, is so much more than the translation can convey: *"Ton nom n'est dans aucun, ta pensée est dans tous"* ("Your name doesn't appear in any, but your essence is in all").

My great-grandfather was thirty-two years old when he married Marie Alasseur in 1894. She was twenty-five. Approximately nine months later, their son Philippe was born in 1895, followed by their daughter (my grandmother, Antoinette), born in 1897. In honor of their twenty-fifth wedding anniversary in 1919, he wrote the poem "Silver Wedding Anniversary."

NOCES D'ARGENT

La barque vogue en paix vers la rive incertaine
Quand le pilote sait éviter les remous,
Et que la passagère, au bout de la carène,
Conduit le gouvernail d'un geste ferme et doux.

Accorder ses efforts, c'est la règle certaine
Pour n'être pas un jour brisés sur les cailloux.

La barque vogue en paix vers la rive incertaine
Quand le pilote sait éviter les remous.

Cet accord de deux cœurs dans l'affection sereine
Nous l'avons conservé avec un soin jaloux
Et depuis vingt-cinq ans, dans la joie et la peine,
Dans les déceptions, les chagrins, les à-coups,
La barque vogue en paix vers la rive incertaine.

7 Juin 1919

SILVER WEDDING ANNIVERSARY

A boat will sail peacefully along an uncertain shore
When the pilot knows how to avoid the eddies,
And the passenger in the stern, furthermore,
Controls the rudder smoothly and firmly.

Coordinating these efforts is an important chore,
The rocks pose an ongoing threat most deadly.
A boat will sail peacefully along an uncertain shore
When the pilot knows how to avoid the eddies.

This accord of two hearts in serene rapport
We have protected with vigilant care,
And so for twenty-five years, in joy and war,
With disappointments, sorrows, wear, and tear,
The boat sails peacefully along an uncertain shore.

June 7, 1919

Using an apt metaphor of a boat for their marriage, he emphasizes the importance of the crew working together under perilous conditions to ensure their safety. Displaying the social dynamics of the time, he is the pilot of the vessel, setting the course and navigating the dangers. He refers to her as a "passenger" (*passagère*) in the back of the boat, but stresses the importance of her role: controlling the rudder "smoothly and firmly." My great-grandmother may not have had the same societal and legal rights as her husband, but family lore has it that she was a competent, strong, equal partner in their marriage.

Together for twenty-five years, they managed through ups and downs to maintain the integrity and direction of their marriage, and the boat continued "to sail peacefully along an uncertain shore." While the poem is somewhat restrained in tone, it appears that the voyage, thus far, had been a success.

"Bon-Papa, share with me some of your family memories."

"I remember fondly the evenings we would spend together discussing literature, reading poetry, and Marie, Antoinette, and Philippe playing musical instruments. Your grandmother sang beautifully and played many instruments, including the cello, which was her favorite. Your great-uncle played the piano and violin, and Marie played the harp, harpsichord, and piano. They were all quite gifted.

"I wrote the poem 'Violin and Cello' after watching them playing their instruments together in the salon. They were amused. These were wonderful moments."

VIOLON ET VIOLONCELLE

Couchés nonchalamment sur le canapé rose
Grand frère et petit frère aiment à rêvasser ;

Mais sur le piano, dès que la main se pose,
On entend l'harmonique en leurs flancs résonner.

Leur âme est en émoi, et, curieuse chose,
Dès qu'ils sont éveillés, se mettent à ronfler.
Couchés nonchalamment sur le canapé rose
Grand frère et petit frère aiment à rêvasser.

Grand frère exhale un chant langoureux et morose
Petit frère, en fausset, se plait à gambader
Et sur un cri aigu, pour terminer, se pose…
Et puis, toujours d'accord, ils vont se reposer
Couchés nonchalamment sur le canapé rose.

VIOLIN AND CELLO

Reclined on the rose-colored sofa nonchalantly,
Big brother and little brother enjoy daydreaming.
But, when hands touch the piano, invariably
Their harmony from within begins resonating.

Their soul is stirring, and curiously,
As they awaken, they begin snoring.
Reclined on the rose-colored sofa nonchalantly,
Big brother and little brother enjoy daydreaming.

Big brother exhales, languid and morose,
Little brother's falsetto frolics happily,
And with a sharp cry, a close, grandiose …
And then together, they rest amicably,
Reclined on the rose-colored sofa nonchalantly.

Among my mother's papers was a concert program for the Alfred Cortot Scholarship Fund held in New York City on May 11, 1938. The program introduces my grandmother— Antoinette Gide, soprano—and Berthe Bert, pianist. One of the pieces they performed was Claude Debussy's *"Clair de lune"* ("Moonlight"), inspired by Paul Verlaine's poetry and featuring lyrics from his poem of the same name. These were two favored artists in my mother's family. I did not know my grandmother, as she passed when I was very young, but listening to this numinous piece of music allowed me to imagine her and envision her spirit as it "mingles with the moonlight" (Verlaine, *"Clair de lune"*).

Paul Verlaine published his poem "Moonlight" in his book *Fêtes galantes, Romances sans paroles,* which I also found in my mother's antique desk.

My grandmother gave this book to my mother on her twentieth birthday with the following dedication:

> *Pour toi, ma chérie, ces précieux poèmes, liés au souvenir des joies que nous eûmes à les interpréter ensemble. Antoinette Gide, 28 juillet 1941.*
>
> For you, my *chérie,* these precious poems, linked to the memory of the joys we had interpreting them together. Antoinette Gide, 28 July 1941.

The language is formal, but it was a very personal gift and a thoughtful dedication. It is a book I reread.

"Bon-Papa, I have a picture taken of Antoinette on her wedding day in January 1919 with Réne Gide that remarkably construes the social milieu, ambiance, time, and place. In the photograph, my grandfather is in uniform, displaying his medals—the *Légion d'honneur* and the *Croix de Guerre*."

"They were a marvelous couple. They were married two months after the war ended. The Great War was shockingly traumatic, but upon its conclusion, life needed to go on. Your grandfather had been injured in the war, receiving shrapnel in the leg. The wound became infected, his skin turned yellow, and his recovery was precarious. I remember that he had difficulty walking and standing."

In the photograph, my grandfather, René Gide, is handsome but obviously unwell. He is thin. His face is drawn, but he is resolute. He is standing, but due to his leg injury, he leans heavily on the couch upon which his young bride sits. He had a limp and walked with a cane for the rest of his life.

My grandmother, Antoinette Gide, is an ethereal beauty in her exquisite white wedding gown of silk and lace. She sits in a salon surrounded by beautiful furniture and *objets d'art*. Ever the artist, her gaze is abstracted and ruminative.

My grandparents were the gilded children of *La Belle Époque*—an era shattered by bellicose statesmen and bungling bureaucrats with hidden agendas and ulterior motives, culminating in the decimation of an entire generation. My grandfather and grandmother would go on to become successful in their respective interests, he as a businessman and she as a patron of the arts in both the United States and France during the 1920s and 1930s. Their son Christian

Gide would, as an officer in the French army, resist the Nazi invasion of France in 1940, escaping to England after France's defeat. He would return with General Charles de Gaulle to liberate Paris in 1944.

"Bon-Papa, I have two sons. How was your relationship with your son, my great-uncle Philippe?"

"I remember his birth vividly. How happy and proud I was. The love a parent feels for a child is unconditional, frightening, and powerful. I wrote the poem 'Fresh! Fresh cheese!' commemorating that day."

A LA CRÈME!
FROMAGE A LA CRÈME!...

Voile de mousseline et petit cœur tout blanc,
Vers la ville s'en va le fromage à la crème
Dans le panier du vieux qui s'éloigne en chantant
Sa plaintive chanson, quand rosit l'aube blême.

Avec un petit pain, il compose souvent
Un somptueux festin au pays de Bohême,
Voile de mousseline et petit cœur tout blanc,
Vers la ville s'en va le fromage à la crème.

Il tremble au moindre heurt, il est tendre, innocent,
Fragile, sans défense, et c'est pourquoi je l'aime.
Dans son berceau d'osier on dirait un enfant
Dormant sur des coussins, en robe de baptême...
Voile de mousseline et petit cœur tout blanc!

Senlis

FRESH!
FRESH CHEESE!...

Veil of muslin and a small white heart
The fresh cheese goes to the city
In the basket of the elder who sings traveling to market
His plaintive song, as the pale dawn grows in intensity.

With a little bread, he often starts
A sumptuous feast in the idyllic country.
Veil of muslin and a small, white heart,
The fresh cheese goes to the city.

With the slightest bump, he trembles, he is innocent,
Fragile, without defense, and that is why I love him.
In his wicker basket, he is like an infant
Sleeping on cushions with baptismal trim...
Veil of muslin and a small white heart!

Senlis

This is one of the few poems in my great-grandfather's collection that exudes unbridled joy. The poem was written in the town of Senlis, located northwest of Paris. My great-grandfather lived there and worked at the courthouse. Philippe Le Molt was born in Senlis. Creating an analogy using his love of simple country traditions and lifestyle, his poem celebrates his son's birth and his homecoming. We can feel his elation in becoming a father and the unconditional love he has for his child. However, their relationship may have been tested.

"But you know, Olivier, my son Philippe and I did have our differences.

"My father was a lawyer, his father, whom I am named for, was a doctor, and my great-grandfather was a judge. Philippe was expected to follow in the family tradition, and he did acquire a law degree. However, he decided to become a painter! It was a bit of a shock."

"I can appreciate that, Bon-Papa, but perhaps, given your poetic nature, you could empathize with your young son's artistic sensibilities."

"I did. Leonardo da Vinci keenly depicts the symmetry between these two art forms: 'Painting is poetry that is seen rather than felt, and poetry is painting that is felt rather than seen.' However, I did not consider being a poet or a painter a practical profession, and I was concerned with the expected lack of pecuniary reward. I wrote my poems during my private hours."

"I understand the concern."

"Of course, Philippe attempted to assuage my concerns with the timeless, and convenient, rationalization of all true artists voiced by the painter Maurice Denis: 'The moment the artist thinks of money, he loses his sense of Beauty.'

"Marie and I supported his decision, and yes, I vicariously enjoyed his dedication to art. However, he also chose an alternative lifestyle, had no interest in marriage, and was very private. It is often better to judge less in familial matters in order to love more.

"After some thought on this, the poem 'The Hanging Gardens' emerged."

LES JARDINS SUSPENDUS

Il est un charme étrange aux jardins suspendus,
Audacieux défi jeté à la matière;
Où l'arbuste se sent perdu
Loin de la terre nourricière.

C'est l'attrait du fruit défendu,
Du chemin sortant de l'ornière.
Il est un charme étrange aux jardins suspendus,
Audacieux défi jeté à la matière.

La fumée enroulant ses anneaux distendus
Monte comme l'encens de l'humble chaumière.
Du coq résonne au loin l'appel inattendu…
L'homme rêve en silence, ivre de lumière.
Il est un charme étrange aux jardins suspendus.

HANGING GARDENS

There is a strange charm to hanging gardens,
A bold challenge issued to standard positions,
Where plants feel lost, suspended,
Far from the Earth's nourishing conditions.

It is the appeal of the fruit forbidden,
The way out of the quotidian.
There is a strange charm to hanging gardens,
A bold challenge issued to standard positions.

The smoke winding in loose rings
From the humble cottage, climbs like incense.
The unexpected echoes of the rooster faraway calling…

The man dreams in silence, in drunken luminescence.
There is a strange charm to hanging gardens.

Philippe Le Molt challenged "standard positions" in his own unique, individual ways. He did enjoy critical success as a figurative painter. Philippe studied under René-Xavier Prinet (Félix Le Molt's first cousin), well known for his painting *The Kreutzer Sonata*. Their works were featured in the French art competition painting event during the 1932 Summer Olympics held in Los Angeles.

Philippe painted landscapes, interiors, and still-lifes characterized by warm colors, soft light, and a relaxed ambiance. He would become a member of a group called the Painters of Poetic Reality. His father would have approved.

A well-regarded art critic of the day, Maurice Brillant, wrote a glowing tribute to Philippe Le Molt's style and personal character in the July/August 1950 edition of the art review publication *Marie*. It seems unlikely that M. Brillant would have been familiar with the introduction written by François Mauriac for Félix Le Molt's book of poems. The descriptive similarities between the two writings are, therefore, all the more striking. Both claim that they were "seduced" and captivated by the musicality of the artistic work of their respective protagonists. They are both impressed with the Le Molts' (*père* et *fils*) reserved and reasonable moral character representing the best of "old France" or the "very heart of France."

My great-grandfather died at the relatively young age of sixty of a ruptured appendix when his son Philippe was twenty-seven. He did not have a chance to witness his son's successes and did not have enough time to know his son as a man and enjoy sharing their similarities and accepting their differences. As a result, Philippe lost the opportunity to present himself on equal footing to his father and, in the process, to more fully develop rapport and mutual respect.

At my father's funeral, I recited the following haiku written by the Japanese poet Sogetsu-Ni (1759–1819), which provided a measure of closure to my truncated father-son relationship:

The sky clears
And the moon and the snow
Are one color.

After the storms have cleared, despite differences, fathers and sons will always have a special bond.

Throughout his life, Philippe Le Molt's paintings were exhibited in major cities around the world, receiving various awards, and the paintings are still being sold today. In 1953, he was awarded the *Légion d'honneur* for his contributions to French culture.

While researching for this book, my sister Nathalie came across a painting of his being sold on eBay. Based on photographs, she recognized the scene as the salon of the family house in Bourbonne-les-Bains ("with a rose-colored couch"). In the corner stood our grandmother's harp. The painting, now hanging in my house, enables me to further enjoy visualizing the evenings the family spent playing music together and reading (and writing) poetry.

Bourbonne-les-Bains was Félix Le Molt's inside world and family sanctuary.

Rouen

The city of Rouen was Félix Le Molt's outside world and his crucible.

My great-grandfather enjoyed studying the past. He believed that the past could guide the present and illuminate the future. The city of Rouen was the perfect campus.

"Many of your poems are set around the ancestral country home in Bourbonne, Bon Papa, but you also write several poems about the city of Rouen. You loved that city, didn't you?"

We walked down deserted narrow cobblestone streets enveloped in a seductive chilling fog. This northern city situated on the river Seine was an important commercial, cultural and political center in Medieval France. Founded by the Gauls two thousand years ago and further developed by the Romans it became the capital of the Duchy of Normandy and home to William the Conqueror. The tomb of the Viking Rollo the first Duke of Normandy as well as the heart of Richard the Lionheart, Duke of Normandy and King of England, are buried here. I could feel the past was an intrinsic part of the present.

"Yes, I was most happy to spend the last twenty years of my life working at the Palais de Justice in Rouen. Such a historic and beautiful building. Rouen itself was a special place with so much history. The city has retained many of its medieval characteristics, with its old wooden houses and neighborhoods, beautiful churches, and special monuments such as the magnificent *Gros Horloge*—the fourteenth-century astronomical clock."

However, modernity was threatening.

Throughout my great-grandfather's poetry, we sense his mourning of a lost era. His world was rapidly changing. Never before had so much change occurred so quickly. The unprecedented increase and disparity in wealth, the changing technology and sociopolitical norms created a vertiginous feeling of accelerating into the unknown. These changes threatened traditional ways of life and, to many, devalued culture and moral sensibilities.

He shares his concern about this situation in the poem "The Future, the Present, the Past," which portrays the future as something humans pursue futilely at the expense of the present and the past. The present leaves no trace, and the past, while reliable, is regrettably stigmatized, so we are left chasing a phantasm.

L'AVENIR, LE PRÉSENT, LE PASSÉ

L'avenir c'est l'oiseau qu'on chasse,
D'autant plus convoité qu'il est moins défini,

Qui vole dans laisser de trace
Et dont personne, hélas! ne découvre le nid.

L'oiseau tombe comme une masse,
C'est le présent brutal qui nait quand il finit;
L'avenir c'est l'oiseau qu'on chasse,
D'autant plus convoité qu'il est moins défini.

Seul le passé n'est pas fugace
Et se fixe dans l'infini,
Mais comme l'oiseau qu'on ramasse,
Le doigt de la mort l'a terni.
L'avenir c'est l'oiseau qu'on chasse…

THE FUTURE, THE PRESENT, THE PAST

The future is the bird we chase,
All the more coveted, being less defined.
It flies without leaving a trace
With a nest, alas! we can never find.

Like a bird that falls heavily in haste,
The brutal present is born and left behind.
The future is the bird we chase,
All the more coveted, being less defined.

Only the past is not impermanent,
Forever fixed in the infinite.
But like a fallen bird unfortunate
The finger of death has tarnished it.
The future is the bird we chase…

"Bon-Papa, you lived in such an interesting time; so much changed during your lifetime! What did you think of all these transformations?"

"I will attempt to explain the societal changes and my sentiments and concerns.

"I identified with the feeling that Charles Péguy provided in his essay, *L'argent.* He writes, 'The world has changed more in the last thirty years than in all the time since Jesus Christ.' A bit overdramatic, but he goes on to capture the essence of a France that had been transformed in less than a decade, with a corresponding loss of culture and tradition."

This excerpt from the essay compellingly captures Péguy's perception of a rapid, unforeseen, and disturbing change:

We were brought up in a whole different world. A child brought up in the city of Orleans between 1873 and 1880 literally lived in ancient France, among its ancient people [and] was, in fact, one of the people of ancient France and part of the old France of the people. Indeed, he was part of it in its entirety, because ancient France was still whole and intact. The collapse happened, if I may say so, all in one piece and in less than a few years.

Péguy corroborates the prevailing mystical undercurrent of emotion that "old France"—its vitality, its beauty, and the uniqueness of its people—had been lost within his lifetime. François Mauriac also feels this emotional pull when he alludes to "old France" in his preface to Félix Le Molt's book of poetry.

The "collapse" Péguy refers to would, of course, lead some factions of society to exploit this sentiment by promoting the conspiracy theory that France's greatness had been stolen by sinister forces.

This emotional perception was reinforced by physical changes. The massive urban renewal of Paris, which began under Napoleon III and was implemented by Georges-Eugène Haussmann, continued during *La Belle Époque*. With urban renovating, old neighborhoods were destroyed, narrow streets lost their charm and became boulevards, and decrepit houses were replaced or eliminated.

"I was concerned that transformations in the city were contributing to a loss of connection to the past. I lamented the loss of old neighborhoods, old ways of life, and a sense of history. Hence, my poem, 'Old Houses.'"

"Old Houses" tugs at the heartstrings by comparing the old rickety houses scheduled to be torn down to neglected grandmothers. The meaningful memories they hold will be replaced by mediocrity and the superficial artificiality of modernity, with its disconnection from the past. He pleads, in his "Envoi," with modern architects (the grand destroyers!) to refrain from their path of destruction.

LES VIELLES MAISONS (EXTRAIT)

Comme des aïeules frileuses,
A l'âtre se chauffant les doigts,
Elles se courbent, douloureuses,
Les branlantes maisons de bois.

ENVOI

Architecte, grand destructeur,
Laisse vivre ces pauvres vieilles.
Tu n'as pas toujours le bonheur
De nous construire des merveilles!

OLD HOUSES (EXCERPT)

Like shivering grandmothers
Warming themselves by the fire,
They bend, aching,
These tired, rickety houses of wood.

ENVOI

Architect, grand destroyer,
Let live these elders.
You don't always have the pleasure
Of building us such wonders!

"But Bon-Papa, surely you acknowledge the need for progress?"

"Olivier, modern man must not lose the ability to connect with his ancestral heritage; otherwise he is but a leaf blown by the wind. We must not lose these historical structures and cultural icons. Our historical perspective. We must appreciate these past achievements and uphold our responsibilities to preserve them. What has been destroyed cannot be replaced by works of equal passion."

"I agree. The English statesman Winston Churchill made a perceptive observation: 'We shape our buildings; thereafter they shape us.' He, too, was concerned with modern design and wanted to preserve architectural traditions."

"I have heard of him. A wise man. Current buildings do not compare with the dignity and aesthetics of the older buildings, and we should not resign ourselves to their destruction. These wonderful structures embody the human spirit."

"I share those sentiments, Bon Papa. However, I must take issue with your poem '*L'impasse Deseveaux*.'"

L'IMPASSE DESEVEAUX

Cette impasse me plaît, tortueuse et vieillotte
Elle s'enfuit, discrète, entre ses murs lépreux.
Tout y est de travers, l'imprévu est sa note,
Et ses jours de souffrance ont un regard peureux.

Au coin des huis moussus tremblote
Dans l'ombre, un liquide douteux;
Cette impasse me plaît, tortueuse et vieillotte
Elle s'enfuit, discrète, entre ses murs lépreux.

C'est là que tiennent leur parlote
Les gueux, les chiens, les amoureux.
Sur sa porte, un rentier, coiffé de sa calotte,
Montre qu'il est facile à l'homme d'être heureux
Cette impasse me plait, tortueuse et vieillotte.

L'IMPASSE DESEVEAUX

This alley pleases me, winding and quaint,
She flees discreetly between its leprous walls.

Everything is crooked, the unexpected awaits,
And its days of suffering have a fearful call.

At the corner of the mossy door oscillates,
In the shadows, a moisture mysterious;
This alley pleases me, winding and quaint,
She flees discreetly between its leprous walls.

It is there they hold their banter,
The beggars, the dogs, and the lovers.
Cap on, at his door, a pensioner
Shows how easy it is for a man to be content.
This alley pleases me, winding and quaint.

"Bon-Papa, these neighborhoods may have seemed pictur-esque to those who had the luxury of not living there. The reality was more pestiferous for the inhabitants without such a choice. 'Leprous walls' and 'mysterious moisture' do not project an inviting habitat. Aren't you romanticizing the pensioner's contentment living in his neighborhood of old crooked houses with their roofs tangled together, hanging over musty, crowded alleys? The existing unsanitary conditions, overcrowding, and impediments to progress needed to be addressed."

"I don't disagree with you, Olivier. Please do not misun-derstand. I simply want to preserve these old neighborhoods, their character, and celebrate their humanity. I acknowledge the need for improvement. But it doesn't have to be all or nothing. Let us not abandon the past. It is uplifting for us all to be able to walk in the footsteps of our forefathers. I envision the old houses and churches being able to not only cohabitate with modernity but enhance it as well!"

"That would create a wonderful synergy, Bon-Papa."

"Yes, and maintaining the memories of the past and relying on its comforting stability enables us to better cope with chaos. A balance is needed. The journalist Raoul Frary provided us this advice: 'The cult of the beautiful must not make us neglect the culture of the useful.'

"I address this potential symbiotic relationship in the poem 'The Goldfish.'"

LE POISSON ROUGE (EXTRAIT)

Ainsi parle dans sa logique
L'homme guidé par la raison,
Et dont la flamme poétique
N'illumine pas l'horizon.
La nature a double visage
Comme Janus, le bi-fronté,
On voit, selon qu'on l'envisage,
L'utilité ou la beauté.

THE GOLDFISH (EXCERPT)

Thus speaks in logic
Man guided by reason
Whose poetic flame melodic
Does not illuminate the horizon.
Nature has a duality,
Like Janus, two-faced deity,

So we see, dependent on how we assay,
Utility or beauty.

"It is truly a joy speaking with you, Bon-Papa. I hope I have not been too annoying."

Out on the Town
With Bon-Papa

"Olivier, we will now be less contemplative. It is time to celebrate! Tonight we go into Paris! In the words of our favorite much-quoted poet Horace, *'NUNC EST BIBENDUM!'* Now is the time for drinking!"

"All right, Bon-Papa, but now you are frightening me."

"I will take you for an experience I enjoyed in Paris before I was married. We will don the clothes of younger men and take the train to Paris from Rouen this evening."

"May I ask where we are going?"

"When we board the train and have a drink in the club car, I will prepare you for tonight's adventure."

The train was a work of art—a steam locomotive of power and beauty, black iron and silver steel. Inside the immaculately maintained polished mahogany wood, leather seats, subtle lighting, and large windows felt opulent and comforting. In the club car, Bon Papa ordered us two Bocks—a strong dark beer. Bon-Papa raised his glass and said:

Nous cherchons fortune
Autour du Chat Noir
Au clair de la lune
A Montmartre, ce soir!

(We seek our fortune
In the moonlight
Le Chat Noir is the one
In Montmartre tonight!)

Le Chat Noir! I had seen the many posters and artwork featuring the sinister black cat but knew little other than it was a famous nightclub in Paris during *La Belle Époque.*

"Going there with you is a dream come true, Bon-Papa. Why is it called 'Le Chat Noir'?"

"The black cat is independent, seductive, mysterious, somewhat frightening, and controversial but also respected and admired. It symbolizes animalistic artistic freedom and individuality. Le Chat Noir attracts poets, artists, and free thinkers. There is a unique dynamic at work. We will be meeting some strange characters, and you will be immersed in a world of interesting artistic and cultural dialogue.

"But I must warn you this crowd is irreverent and ribald, nothing is taken seriously, and everything can and should be mocked."

"I am all in Bon-Papa."

"We will be having dinner there with my childhood friend, the sculptor Léon-Joseph Chavalliaud. Our deep friendship provides us the ability to communicate what is really important to us, thereby heightening our joys and lessening our sorrows. We are much better for it."

"Such a friendship is rare. It is a valuable gift.

"I am looking forward to this experience. Allow me to order another round of Bocks!"

"Thank you. Olivier, to appreciate the experience, it is important to understand that Le Chat Noir portrays itself as a medieval tavern with the expected furniture, tapestries, antiques, and, most importantly, the conviviality. The people who work there speak in old French, or a parody of it. Songs are sung and poetry recited that follow the traditions of medieval troubadours, often off color, sometimes nonsensical, satirical, and insulting. They are meant to provoke you and make you laugh. Plays on words are much admired. *L'esprit gaulois*, the spirit of the Gauls, the early inhabitants of what is now known as France, is also celebrated. The founder Rodolphe Salis is quite eccentric."

"I have read, Bon-Papa, that this attraction to things medieval was very much in vogue during your time."

"Yes, an expansive interest in the Middle Ages developed in reaction to the malaise that afflicted France. Le Chat Noir exploited this sentiment. It provided a reassuring environment to retreat into an idealized image of the France of the Middle Ages. We could imagine a past that seemingly offered unity, certainty, and greatness. The myth was appealing."

As we approached Le Chat Noir, a tall Swiss guard traditionally attired in blue, red, orange, and yellow stood guard at the entrance armed with an even taller halberd. "To bar any priests and creditors from entry," whispered Bon-Papa. Hanging overhead was a large metal sign with the famous black cat appearing startled, perched on a crescent moon. To the left of the door hung a sign:

"PASSERBY STOP! THIS ESTABLISHMENT, BY THE WILL OF FATE, WAS CONSECRATED, UNDER THE AUSPICES OF LE CHAT NOIR, TO THE MUSES AND TO JOY. PASSERBY, BE MODERN."

"Be modern in a medieval tavern? What does that mean?" I inquired.

"Demonstrate your individuality. Be yourself. Enjoy life to the fullest. Ah, here is Léon."

The three of us stepped inside. Large tapestries with nature motifs hung on the walls. A stuffed boar's head overlooked the room from above a huge fireplace in which tree trunks seemed to be burning. A human skull was displayed on the mantle. The room was filled with raucous conversation and laughter. On one side, a piano was playing, barely audible above the din. On the other side, a troubadour was singing accompanied by a *guiterne*, a small guitar-like instrument. I liked the ambiance. This could be interesting, I thought.

Ahead of us, a dignified older couple was being greeted by a robust, animated middle-aged man wearing an elegant cravat and floral satin doublet under a dark coat. "That is Salis," whispered Bon-Papa.

"Welcome, my Lord Most Distinguished! How wonderful you could bring your charming wife this time! By the way, what happened to that enchanting young thing from the other night? Come, let me show you to your table."

We were next.

"Such handsome young gentlemen! Lord Le Molt, it has been such a long time! I hear you are on your way to becoming a high and mighty judge. How wonderful it is that you grace our humble establishment. Let me assure you that I am totally innocent of my many crimes and will provide you with as much alcohol as you may need to convince yourself of that fact! I have a special table for you and your friends!"

We sat at a table with a view of the entire room. "Shall I order us vermouth with oysters and caviar?" proposed Léon.

"Thank you, Léon. I have been told that you are a sculptor. Sculptures are my favorite visual art form. I so love Michelangelo's expressive assertion that he is simply releasing the sculpture from its captivity within the marble block. It has always been there. It is up to you, Master sculptor, to discover it!"

"I do admire that imaginative instinctive approach. What drew me to this art form is its multidimensional nature. It is so expressive. I recently completed a monument in Brittany and will be going to England to work on various projects."

Bon-Papa joined in. "On my twenty-second birthday, Léon presented me, as a token of friendship, a bust representing my likeness. On the left shoulder, he signed the inscription

'To my friend F. Le Molt,' and on the right shoulder is 'Paris 1884.' Quite marvelous. I enjoy it very much."

"How wonderful to hear of your camaraderie. Léon, as you know, Félix is a very private person, but I will reveal to you that he is also an artist. He is a poet!"

"Really, Félix! Please recite one of your poems for us."

"All right. The vermouth has given me courage, so voilà...."

"LE CHEMIN CREUX

Qu'il est joli, le chemin creux,
Semé de fleurs, bordé d'orties,
Qui s'en va, mince et tortueux
Par les guérets et les prairies!

Que m'importe qu'il soit boueux
Les jours où le vient voir la pluie;
Il est joli, le chemin creux,
Semé de fleurs, bordé d'orties.

Là-haut, n'a-t-on pas le ciel bleu?
Et puis, quand l'ornière est franchie,
Le mauvais pas n'est plus qu'un jeu.
C'est là l'image de la vie...
Suivons gaîment son chemin creux. "

(THE SUNKEN TRAIL

The sunken trail is so alluring,
Bordered in nettles, sown with flowers.
Who goes on its way, slender and winding
By the fields, tillage and pastures!

Who cares if they are muddying
On the days of rain showers?
The sunken trail is so alluring,
Bordered in nettles, sown with flowers.

Above, do we not have a blue sky endearing?
And when a rut is confronted,
The bad step is part of the undertaking.
Here is life represented …
Let's gaily follow its sunken trail so alluring.)

"Magnifique, mon cher Félix! To life! How I have missed you, Félix."

"And I you, Léon. Our friendship is for the ages."

"Did I hear poetry being recited at this table?" interjected the troubadour, who seemed to be everywhere at once. "Since you apparently can appreciate the art, if not compose it properly, allow me to regale you with a real poem compliments of Paul Verlaine, who sits across the room.

"Dansons la gigue!

J'aimais surtout ses jolis yeux
Plus clairs que l'étoile des cieux,
J'aimais ses yeux malicieux.

Dansons la gigue!

Elle avait des façons vraiment
De désoler un pauvre amant,
Que c'en était vraiment charmant!

Dansons la gigue!

Mais je trouve encore meilleur
Le baiser de sa bouche en fleur
Depuis qu'elle est morte à mon cœur.

Dansons la gigue!

Je me souviens, je me souviens
Des heures et des entretiens,
Et c'est le meilleur de mes biens.

Dansons la gigue!

(Let's dance a jig!

I loved, above all, her pretty eyes
Brighter than stars in the skies,
I loved her malicious eyes likewise.

Let's dance a jig!

She for sure, she knew the art
Of breaking a poor lover's heart,
How charmingly she played the part.

Let's dance a jig!

But I find it even better
That kiss of her mouth in flower
Now, in my heart, she's a dead letter.

Let's dance a jig!

I recall, oh I recall
The hours, the words we let fall,
And this the very best of all.

Let's dance a jig!
Translation: A. S. Kline)

"Another round of vermouth for this table of struggling artists!" shouted the troubadour.

We thanked him, complimenting him on his delivery. Bon-Papa gave him a *pourboire* (a tip). The French word literally means to enable someone to buy a drink. The troubadour had earned it.

Paul Verlaine was indeed in the room. I saw him slouched in a corner, apparently asleep. Léon made a drinking gesture, insinuating that our *poète maudite* had had too much to drink.

We noticed a commotion at the door. "The Hydropaths have arrived," Bon-Papa informed us.

"And there is Emile Goudeau, the founder," added Léon. "The Hydropaths are a literary club. Goudeau is also editor of the journal *Le Chat Noir*. Written in Old French, it features medieval legends, history, songs, and poetry using the rondeau format."

I noticed the gregarious, intense, brown-skinned man with very black hair and beard holding court with half a dozen friends and bantering with Salis.

"What is the significance of their name?" I asked.

"Hydropath refers to people who dislike water. The members of this group only drink alcohol, and they are prodigious drinkers! They proclaim that their only doctrine is not having one. They state that there is only one ultimate judge or Supreme Court of their talents—posterity—but that it is rarely in session during the author's lifetime!" chuckled Bon-Papa.

"Félix, I am sure they will soon be joined tonight by other clubs, such as the Jemenfoutistes, and the Zutistes."

Interested, I inquired how one goes about becoming a member of these clubs.

Léon responded, "Essentially Olivier, as their names imply, you can only drink alcohol, cannot give a damn, and you must express disdain and disbelief about everything. They don't have particularly difficult entry requirements."

I shook my head and laughed.

Bon-Papa (wearing the clothes of a younger man) made an observation:

"The waitress has beautiful eyes."

"Despite your proper intellectual and philosophical façade, you are, at heart, *mon cher* Félix, a romantic!"

"Léon, have you seen the opera *Manon?*"

"No, tell me about it."

"It is a chivalric tale of star-crossed lovers. And yes, it does exhibit my longing for bygone, more romantic days. I confess to falling in love with Manon, the heroine of the opera. I wrote a poem after watching the performance. Would you like to hear part of it?"

Léon looked at me. "Olivier, I don't think we can stop him, do you?"

Bon-Papa ignored us:

"De l'époque héroïque on n'a plus la manière,
Finis les coups d'estoc, finis les songe-creux!
Manon participe aux retraites ouvrières,
Et seuls, quelques rêveurs chantent en vers boiteux
Dans la blancheur du lait, l'œil noir de la laitière!"

(No longer do we live in such a heroic age.
Gone the cut and thrust, gone the romantics!
Manon now receives the workers' wages,
And few, the dreamers, sing with shaky lyrics
Of the whiteness of the milk, the dark eyes of the
milkmaid!)

The wandering troubadour couldn't resist jumping in.

"I am a romantic, too! I will prove it courtesy of Victor Hugo …

La vie est une fleur,
L'amour en est le miel
C'est la colombe unie
A l'aigle dans le ciel,

C'est la grâce tremblante
à la force appuyée,
C'est ta main dans ma main
doucement oubliée."

(Life is a flower
love is its honey.
It is the dove united
with the eagle in the sky,

It is trembling grace
with sustained force,
It's your hand in my hand
gently forgotten.)

We all had to agree that the troubadour was indeed quite the romantic.

"In the interest of living a life with passion, allow me to offer you both a toast," I suggested. "In the words of the poet Baudelaire, 'Get drunk. One should always be drunk. That's all that matters; that's our one imperative need. With wine, with poetry, with virtue as you choose. But get drunk.'"

"Well said" my companions chorused. We drained our glasses.

"No more vermouth," exclaimed Léon. "We must start drinking absinthe!"

"Yes," agreed Bon-Papa. "Before the show starts."

"First, what is absinthe, and second, what show?" I asked.

Léon and Bon-Papa looked at each other and laughed.

"*La Fée Verte* (the Green Fairy). You have never had absinthe, Olivier?" asked Léon. "You are in for a treat. It is a green poison most vile. You must try it."

Despite my semi-inebriated state, I still realized that those statements did not make much sense, but when in Le Chat Noir…

Three glasses arrived with a sugar cube placed on a slotted spoon on each glass. We were given ice water to pour over the sugar cube, and the water would drip into the glass. The contents turned milky and released a lovely herbal aroma. While indeed vile (and highly alcoholic), the drink did possess a strange seductiveness.

"Now we are ready for the show," said a most content Bon-Papa.

"On the stage in front of us, Olivier, we are going to see a drama unfold called *L'Épopée* (the Epic). It is a retelling of Napoleonic history, especially the great battles, by means of paintings and zinc plates drawn, backlit, and projected against various backgrounds. Very unique and creative," explained Bon-Papa.

Indeed, it was compelling, as was the audience participation. There was much animated shouting and commentary. The absinthe definitely heightened the experience. I concluded that the Green Fairy's popularity was due to a hallucinogenic effect it seemed to produce… or maybe it was its combination with a few too many Bocks and vermouths. In any event, I was in a happy place.

The show ended, but the evening festivities were just beginning. However, we needed to catch the last train back to Rouen. We settled our account, thanked our waitress and troubadour, and put on our coats.

I can only blame the absinthe, that diabolic concoction, for what happened next, for inciting me to do something so out of character. I removed the human skull from the mantel, stood on a chair, and proclaimed to the room:

"Alas, poor Yorick! I knew him, a fellow
of infinite jest, of most excellent fancy: he hath
borne me on his back a thousand times; and now, how
abhorred in my imagination it is! Where be your gibes now? Your
gambols? Your songs? Your flashes of merriment,
that were wont to set the table on a roar?"

I kissed the skull on top of its head and returned it to its proper resting place. The room clapped and roared. Salis, with hands on his hips, smiled and winked.

It hardly mattered that I was reciting incomprehensible Shakespearean English. What was appreciated was the panache, the élan, and the demonstration of a *joie de vivre* accentuated by a poetic performance.

"*Bonne nuit tout le monde, sois moderne! À la prochaine!*" I saluted and walked out the door.

We said our farewells at the train station. Léon was heading for Reims.

Bon-Papa and Léon enveloped each other warmly.

"Léon, we are twins, and together we embrace the eternal."

"Félix, we will always be together running with the stars."

After boarding the train, we settled into our comfortable seats. Within a few minutes, the rhythmic motion and copious alcohol had put Bon-Papa to sleep. I looked out the window and thought of a poem from *La Vie qui passe*:

ENTRE PARIS ET ROUEN, LA NUIT
PAR LA PORTIERE DU WAGON

Au sein mystérieux des plaines endormies
S'allument, une à une, en des obscurs lointains
Les lampes des hameaux, étoiles assoupies
Qui contemplent le ciel d'un regard incertain.

Lampes, vous attestez que subsiste la vie,
Qu'il reste encore du feu dans l'âtre qui s'éteint.
Au sein mystérieux des plaines endormies
Vous piquez vos clous d'or dans des obscurs lointains.

Mais voilà que la lune, au ras des saules, brille,
Et la Seine revêt sa cuirasse d'étain;
Par les monts et les bois, étrange Walkyrie,
Poursuivant dans la nuit son éternel destin
Au sein mystérieux des plaines endormies.

BETWEEN PARIS AND ROUEN,
NIGHT THROUGH THE TRAIN CAR WINDOW

All across the mysteriously sleeping prairie,
Alight, one by one, in the obscure distance,
The lights of the hamlets, as stars drowsy
That contemplate the sky with hesitance.

Glowing lights, you confirm life's vitality.
The dying hearth fires confirm its existence.
All across the mysteriously sleeping prairie,
Your golden nails pierce through the distance.

But now the moon against the willows shines,
And the Seine dons its armor silvery.

Through the hills and woods, a strange Valkyrie,
Pursuing in the night its eternal destiny,
All across the mysteriously sleeping prairie.

This poem has a mystical beauty. I observed the hamlets in the countryside with their faint glowing lights (piercing golden nails) and felt the spiritual pull of the landscape flashing by. We and the train were only passing through and would soon be gone, but I was reassured that life was calmly enfolding all around me in the distance as it should, as it has for many generations. I was at peace.

Faith

"Olivier, let us leave the cities. Come back with me to the church in the center of Bourbonne. We will discuss the importance of religion in my life, and I will share some family history with you."

"Wonderful, Bon-Papa. Many of your poems celebrate the Roman Catholic faith. I noticed that your poems span the spectrum of New Testament Roman Catholic Christian dogma."

"Indeed, and I must stress to you how fundamental French churches and cathedrals were for our culture. They held French society together and became a symbolic connection between the present and the past, creating a sense of continuity."

"Do you think, Bon-Papa, that this connection became even more important during your lifetime?"

"Yes, churches could offer a symbolic return to an era that had seemed more stable, hierarchical, and integrated—an ordered world that could blunt the trauma of modernity.

"Behold the Church of Our Lady of the Assumption here in Bourbonne-Les-Bains Olivier! This church was built in the twelfth century and is a good example of the Gothic style."

"Unquestionably, Bon-Papa, this is quite an imposing stone structure. The vast interior space and height, along with the large stained glass windows, maximize the effect of light. Such a beautiful rose window over the large wooden doors! All of these combine to prompt emotional responses of security as well as awe and wonder."

"My religious passion and devotion are awakened by the sounds of the church bells and plainchant, the beauty of the stained-glass windows, the moods created by the shifting light, the peaceful gardens, and the smell of incense and candles. These vivid sensory triggers flood me with spiritual contentment."

"I am drawn to your emotional attachment to these embodiments of religious faith and French culture, Bon-Papa. Your poem 'The Stained-Glass Windows of Saint-Godard' is quite moving. You exhibit your affinity for cathedrals, their art, their beauty, and the mysterious allure of stained-glass windows."

LES VITRAUX DE SAINT GODARD ÉCLAIRÉS LA NUIT (EXTRAIT)

Le temps a patiné les ors et les opales,
La pourpre a des éclats par les ans assouplis;
J'aime les tons très doux vitraux assombris
Qui brillent dans la nuit aux flancs des Cathédrales.

THE STAINED GLASS WINDOWS OF SAINT GODARD SHINING AT NIGHT (EXCERPT)

The golds and opals, time has blackened,
The purple brightness suffers from aged plight.

I love the soft shades of the windows darkened
That glow from the sides of the cathedral at night.

"France has so many beautiful churches. Beyond its beauty, this church in Bourbonne has been an important part of our family for generations. My grandfather, the doctor, came to Bourbonne to work at the thermal spa. He married my grandmother in 1821 here in this church. My father was baptized here, as I was. You may not know it, but your mother was also baptized here in 1921. Unfortunately, we did not have the opportunity to know each other. Marie, your great-grandmother, would play the organ here during Sunday services."

"I didn't know all that. How fascinating that so many of our generations have passed through this church. I can visualize you and the rest of my mother's family gathered at the marble baptismal basin. These rituals provide that sense of community and continuity.

"It is evident from your poetry, Bon-Papa, that these teachings and beliefs had a powerful influence on your life."

Overwhelmingly, Félix Le Molt's religious poems project Christianity and Catholic institutions as bastions of stability and solace, conveying comfort, beauty, and hope.

LE JARDIN DU CURÉ

Un jardin pacifique orne le presbytère
Qu'étreint un chèvrefeuille aux bras capricieux;
Entr'ouvert, sur un banc, bâille le bréviaire
Près duquel, au soleil, s'étire un chat frileux.

La main dans la ceinture, auprès de son vicaire,
Le curé voit mûrir l'abricot savoureux;
Un jardin pacifique orne le presbytère
Qu'étreint un chèvrefeuille aux bras capricieux.

Le fossoyeur, lassé, quitte le cimetière
Pour planter des radis. Sous un platane ombreux
La vierge au doux sourire étend ses mains de mère
Et verse l'espérance au cœur des malheureux…
Un jardin pacifique orne le presbytère.

THE PRIEST'S GARDEN

A peaceful garden adorns the presbytery
Embraced by a wide-armed honeysuckle tree;
Half-opened, on a bench, yawns the breviary
Near which, in the sun, stretches a cat lazily.

With hand on his rope belt, alongside his vicar,
The priest watches the apricots ripen with scrutiny.
A peaceful garden adorns the presbytery
Embraced by a wide-armed honeysuckle tree.

The gravedigger wearily leaves the cemetery
To plant his radishes. Under a shady sycamore,
The Virgin, with a soft smile, extends her hospitality
And pours hope into the heart of the unfortunate poor…
A peaceful garden adorns the presbytery.

"I grew up like most French children with the unassailable belief that our Catholic faith was an integral part of our identity. The thousand-year historical, cultural, and political association between the French government, the French people, and the Roman Catholic Church created deep roots.

"I felt a sense of comfort that my family's religious and cultural beliefs were unquestionable. These early indoctrinations of beliefs and traditions maintain powerful dominions even later in life, despite their lack of rationality."

We stopped for lunch at a corner café. We sat outside facing a small plaza, appreciating the sun and light breeze. Bon-Papa ordered the potato and leek soup, and I requested the beet salad. We each had a glass of white wine. We quietly digested our lunch, along with the thoughts we had shared. We finished with a cup of coffee.

We resumed our walk.

"Bon-Papa, you tell us in your poem 'The Hours of the Night' that the famous clock near the Hall of Justice in Rouen 'having struck the Maid's death knell, cries in regret!' How incredible and convoluted is the story of Joan of Arc."

Joan of Arc, the Maid of Orleans, was instrumental in revitalizing the fortunes of the French army, enabling them to eventually repel the English invaders during the Hundred Years War. Due to her insistence that she was following instructions from voices sent by God, she was condemned in 1431 as a heretic. Imprisoned near the courthouse in Rouen where my great-grandfather worked, she was tried and convicted by the Roman Catholic Church and burned alive. After the French victory twenty-five years later, her spiritual fortunes were revived. The Church declared her a martyr, and she became a

French national symbol. Joan of Arc was canonized in 1920 and is one of the patron saints of France.

"This is true, Olivier. The histories of the Catholic Church and France are much interwoven and shockingly manipulative and adversarial at times. During my life, those ties finally began to unravel. The Church's control over society was challenged by Protestantism, modernity, and secularization.

"I wanted to believe in the promise of Christianity—with its benevolence of the will of God, as determined by the Roman Catholic Church," asserted my great-grandfather.

"However, I did support the law on the separation of church and state in 1905. The inherent, tempting dangers of using religion as a political tool have had much historical precedent. To some, the passage of this law meant that Modern France had chosen to abandon the Church, thereby unleashing an inevitable, irreparable breakdown of social moral standards."

"Bon-Papa, the United States had codified this separation 114 years earlier in the Bill of Rights. The First Amendment was intended to liberate American citizens from the tyranny of imposed religious beliefs. While the separation of church and state has now been largely accepted by European countries, unfortunately, it has once again become a divisive issue in the United States."

"Olivier, for a country to progress, this separation is vital. Religious beliefs must be personal, not political.

"Despite my deeply felt emotions, I intellectually questioned my personal religious beliefs. No amount of belief makes something a fact. I came to believe that an honest skeptic was closer to God than a dishonest believer. Nature has given us the ability to reason. We are not merely spectators but interpreters. A real seeker of truth must doubt."

Our extended conversation and walk had taken us to the gates of a cemetery. Bon-Papa was pensive as he walked slowly toward a grouping of gravestones. He stopped and extended his arm.

"Olivier, here my father and grandfather rest. There is no greater reminder than this of our mortality. We are provoked into demanding answers for the unknowable. We want control and certainty.

"This is what religious dogmas provide—feelings of control and certainty. However, religion purports to provide certainty but without verifiable proof.

"I confess that I have moments of doubt."

Doubt

"To paraphrase Dante Alighieri and his *Divine Comedy*, midway through the journey of my life, I found myself in a dark wood. I questioned my religious beliefs."

"That is clear, Bon-Papa. Your poem '*Le vent*' ('The Wind') expresses the disquietude found in the Biblical Book of Job."

The poem refers to the wind as the breath and essence of the Judeo-Christian God in Genesis, as it moves across the waters. The wind is often used as a metaphor for the divine because it is intangible, invisible, inexplicable, capricious, and powerful. While wind can never be seen, its actions are felt. Examples are given of the wind's duality—it can be frightening or soothing, wreak havoc or be playful, sadistic, or kind.

LE VENT (EXTRAIT)

Vent, qui es-tu? Dieu ou Démon
Toi dont la voix sans cesse clame,
Faut-il te mettre au Panthéon?
Est-ce l'enfer qui te réclame?

Vent, qui es-tu?...

Pour certains, tu es un grand dieu,
Quand tu t'élèves, tout s'abaisse;
Au loin s'enténèbrent les cieux,
Toute force devient faiblesse.
Peut-être aussi, quand incompris
Serais-tu fait des âmes lasses
D'errer autour du Paradis
Et qui doivent y trouver place;
Ou bien, ce qui serait trop haut
Pour que notre âme s'y apaise,
Cet esprit voguant sur les eaux
Au temps lointain de la Genèse?

Vent, qui es-tu?...

WIND (EXCERPT)

Wind, who are you? God or Devil,
You with voice unrelenting,
Should you be honored in the Pantheon as special?
Is hell demanding a reclaiming?

Wind, who are you?

For some, a great god harkens.
When you rise, all stoop and quail;
In the far distance, skies darken,
All power becomes frail.
Maybe, too, misunderstood mysteriously,
Might you comprise the weary souls,
Who in Paradise wander aimlessly,
Searching for meaning, wanting to be whole;

Or perhaps you are above understanding
Unable to help our souls find solace,
This spirit blown across the waters meandering
Since the faraway time of Genesis?

Wind, who are you?

The poem challenges and questions the wind's nature, much as the Biblical figure Job questioned and challenged God. The poem, with its opening line, "Wind, who are you? God or Devil," invokes the irreverent unease Job felt as he questioned God's morality. "Wind, who you are?" is repeated seven times in "Le Vent," in evident frustration and confusion.

The biblical Book of Job begins with the story of the devout, good man Job, who has a loving family and enjoys a successful, prosperous life. In the Bible, God boasts to Satan about how loyal and pious Job is. Satan questions whether Job would be so devoted if God allowed Satan to destroy Job's well-being. God takes up the challenge and allows Satan's assault on Job. Immediately, a calamitous wind comes roaring out of the desert, killing all of Job's children. His possessions are lost, and Job's health is ruined.

Job maintains his devotion, but he asks God how and why He could have done such a thing. God, responding in the form of a whirlwind, blusters and bullies, essentially telling Job that he is not to question why; he must simply submit. Job's trust in God has been violated, but he must accept that the world lacks the moral order that he, in his limited capacity, had understood it.

"Yes, Olivier, much like the Book of Job, 'The Wind' ends with an underlying, anxious acquiescence that reveals our greatest fears and most difficult struggles: 'Perhaps you are above understanding, unable to help our souls find solace.'

"In my library, I had a copy of Ernest Renan's autobiography *Souvenirs d'Enfance et de Jeunenesse (Recollections of my Youth)*. Renan was considered an important historian, philologist, and religious philosopher in my time. He questioned Christian dogma writing, 'The grains of sand of my doubts accumulated into a solid mass.' Renan also wrote extensively about the Book of Job."

"I am now the proud conservator of that book, Bon-Papa. His influence upon you is evident. In 'The Wind,' you are clearly searching. Your poems interweave the Christian doctrines of faith and redemption on the one hand, and the Greco-Roman philosophy of reason and of living without anxiety on the other."

"Ultimately, Olivier, I sought what the Greek philosopher Epicurus would call *ataraxia,* tranquility achieved with freedom from fear."

"Bon-Papa, in my mother's living room, there hung a portrait of you attired in your robes and judicial finery. You are depicted in the youth of old age, looking fully professionally accomplished. You are standing at a window with the impressive Palais de Justice as a backdrop. Alongside you is a desk embossed with the Le Molt family crest—sheep on a green field with three silver crescents in a blue sky.

"Also embossed on the desk, there is a motto in Latin: NEC SPE NEC METU (NEITHER HOPE NOR FEAR). Please interpret what this saying means to you."

"That was my official portrait as a judge. The artist was quite kind to me. I look younger and thinner, and I have more hair."

"Your beard and mustache are reminiscent of the days of the three musketeers and Cardinal Richelieu! Quite dashing."

"Thank you. I think I'm starting to like you."

We laughed.

"This saying conveys the message that while hope and fear are necessary emotions, we cannot be excessively dependent upon hope nor can we allow ourselves to be dominated by fear. We suffer when we want things to be other than what they are. Both sentiments reflect our perceived lack of control.

"While seemingly opposed to each other, there is in fact a symbiotic relationship between hope and fear—they are intertwined. Our well-being is determined by finding and using the right balance. Undue fantasizing or fearing the future diminishes our ability to live fully in the present."

"But isn't hope a foundation of Christianity?"

"Yes, Olivier. It is the fear of death and the unknown that created the hope of Christianity, but instead of focusing on hope and fear, let us focus on improving our character.

"The Roman emperor and philosopher Marcus Aurelius explains that we should not worry about what the gods think of us because if there are gods and they are just, they will not care how much we worship them but will evaluate us on our character and the virtues we have lived by. If there are gods and they are unjust and capricious, then we will have wasted our time fearing and worshipping them hoping for acceptance. If there are no gods, then we will have lived a good life, done the right things, and will be remembered. Simply strive to live a noble life."

Placing the motto NEC SPE NEC METU in such a conspicuous position in his official portrait was a deliberate act and made a bold and potentially controversial statement. Definitely not a "standard position," this chosen motto reveals the complex and independent thinking of Félix Le Molt.

"However, the tenets of Christianity and Greco-Roman thought are not mutually exclusive, Olivier. They are both vital approaches to living a thoughtful life."

"Bon-Papa, I admire your ability to cultivate an open mind capable of holding multiple philosophical and spiritual approaches to life."

"Life and death are interwoven, and we shouldn't live our lives in fear but rather in serenity, as Nature will continue."

Félix Le Molt had reconciled his beliefs and acquired the comfort and serenity that comes with a deliberate embrace of what fate decides, including suffering and loss and the understanding that everything is continually in the process of becoming; that which has just ended simply marks a new beginning.

The Russian symbolist poet of *La Belle Époque*, Konstantin Balmont, articulated this concept succinctly: "With every instant, I am consumed / In every change, I am reborn."

Félix Le Molt provides us with this reassurance:

LES HEURES SONNENT DANS LA NUIT (EXTRAIT)

Tous ces chants peu à peu s'éloignent lentement
Leur vol harmonieux s'élargit et s'efface
Comme un brouillard léger sous le souffle du vent,
Comme l'ombre qui suit le nuage qui passe.
Le chien reprend son somme et l'homme épouvanté
Songe au temps qui poursuit sa course aventureuse.
La nuit, dans la douceur et la sérénité
Sur la ville s'étend, calme et silencieuse ....

THE HOURS RINGING IN THE NIGHT (EXCERPT)

All these songs slowly dissipate,
Their harmonious journey widens and clears
Like a light fog under a breath of wind evaporates,
Like a shadow that disappears.
The dog resumes its nap, and man with anxiety
Contemplates Time, which continues its adventurous journey.
The night in softness and serenity
Envelopes the town, calmly and quietly ....

Spiritually, Félix Le Molt had made progress toward achieving *ataraxia*, but there were other conflicts to resolve.

The Law

There is a troubling poem in my great-grandfather's book that evinces personal and professional struggles. The poem indicates deep resentment and feelings of betrayal and martyrdom. His poem "The Owl" is transparently autobiographical and brutally graphic in its depictions of suffering endured.

LA CHOUETTE (EXTRAIT)

Pauvre oiseau méconnu! En cherchant l'idéal
Tu irrites les gens qui vivent dans la fange;
Ne te comprenant pas, le paysan brutal
Par les ailes te cloue aux portes de sa grange:
Etre crucifié n'est-ce pas de tout temps
Le sort des incompris? ....

Grand-Couronne 1920

THE OWL (EXCERPT)

Poor misunderstood bird! In searching for the pleasant
You bother the people who live mired on the farm.
Misunderstanding you, the brutish peasant

113

Nails you by your wings to the doors of his barn.
Being crucified, is not that the fate
Of all the misunderstood? ....

Grand-Couronne 1920

In Greek mythology, the owl represented wisdom. In this poem, the owl and its wisdom are misunderstood by "the brutish peasant" and crucified to his barn door. My great-grandfather commiserates with the owl's predicament. The descriptive word "misunderstood" may have been a euphemism for Attorney and Judge Félix Le Molt having been perceived as a provocateur within his profession.

I stood at the gates of the Palais de Justice, waiting for my great-grandfather to exit the building. Built in the early 1500s, it is a magnificent structure worthy of its purpose—a Gothic masterpiece, ornate, but serious in appearance. I would take the tour at some other time.

Bon-Papa took me by the arm and suggested having a coffee down the street. We found a bistro on a town square surrounded by the iconic half-timbered buildings of Normandy. We sat diagonally across from the Fontaine de la Croix de Pierre. Bon-Papa gave me some Rouen history.

"Originally, around the year 1200, a stone cross was consecrated where the fountain now stands. During the religious war of the 1500s, it was destroyed by the Protestants. It was rebuilt in the early 1800s and was recently further restored by a local Rouennais sculptor. A notable monument. What would you like to drink, Olivier?"

It was too late in the day for coffee. I looked forward to a glass of wine. I was also apprehensive, given my proposed line of questioning. My great-grandfather seemed a bit preoccupied. I wasn't sure if that bode well. I opened the conversation softly.

"As a *juge d'instruction*, Bon-Papa, you played an important role in the workings of the court. How challenging that must have been."

"I very much respected and enjoyed practicing law, and I was always aware of the importance of my responsibilities. However, I was at odds throughout my career with many of my colleagues. I was attacked for holding others to a higher standard, for suggesting reforms and resisting corruption."

His poem "The Judges" emanates blatant contempt for his fellow judges and the current legal process. The subtitle "A Courtroom Sketch" sets us up for biting sarcasm and imparts the comedic social commentary of a play by Molière. A scene is portrayed of three judges who are far from being hard at work fulfilling their civic duty and dispensing the wisdom and justice society so desperately needs.

LES JUGES (croquis d'audience)

Sur leurs larges fauteuils, les trois juges assis
Ont l'abord dédaigneux de seigneurs d'importance;
Les voleurs, les escrocs, les amoureux transis,
La dame trop soumise, occupent l'audience.

Leur œil clos, par moments, sort de sa somnolence
Pour jeter dans la salle un regard indécis.

Sur leurs larges fauteuils, les trois juges assis
Ont l'abord dédaigneux de seigneurs d'importance.

Qu'on juge un sacristain ou bien un circoncis,
Que le fait soit douteux ou de jurisprudence,
Qu'un homme ait maraudé, qu'un enfant soit occis,
Digérant doucement, ils dorment en cadence
Sur leurs larges fauteuils, les trois juges assis.

THE JUDGES (a courtroom sketch)

In their large armchairs, the three judges consider,
With the scornful look of important nobility,
The thieves, the swindlers, the nervous lovers,
The downtrodden woman—all attract scrutiny.

Eyes half-closed, they occasionally stir,
Fitfully observing the hall indecisively.
In their large armchairs, the three judges consider,
With the scornful look of important nobility.

Whether judging a cleric or a sinner,
Whether the facts are in doubt or discovered,
Whether a man vandalized or injured a minor,
Digesting tranquilly, they sleep together,
In their large armchairs, the three judges consider.

The poem is an indictment of judges who have abdicated their responsibilities and of the system that perpetuates this dereliction of duty. The judges sit on their thrones imperiously, full of self-importance and contempt for the riffraff in their courtroom. They have illusions of being great nobles of privilege and feel that such a process is beneath them. With "eyes half-closed," they are barely present, and their arrogance and incompetence are evident. No matter how important or upsetting the cases, they quietly digest their large midday meals and nap comfortably.

"Bon-Papa, your poem 'The Judges' is quite harsh. How angry and frustrated you must have been."

"I was. In many ways, the justice system did not rise to the challenges of the period and needed reform. A good judge rules the soul with the soul. A society's justice system reflects the society itself. Society was undergoing radical changes, but the judicial system couldn't adapt."

"What were some of the problems of the legal system?"

"The courts were biased against the defendants and subject to political and societal pressures. The rich, powerful, and connected were above the law. The judges often acted as prosecutors, questioning the defendants themselves. They could tip the scale of justice very easily by announcing their own opinions. The presiding judges were all too quick to become impatient and disparaging, dismissing witnesses they prejudged as being of dubious morality. Juries had limited access to information and were much less educated and socially inferior to courtroom officials. Thus, they were easily swayed. Conviction rates were very high, and unfairly so."

"I read, Bon-Papa, that France's traditional, rural way of life was ending, and this exacerbated the problems of urbanization. People became less rooted. Along with urban growth came the growth of the urban poor, with a resulting increase in crime."

"The newspaper *L'Humanité* proclaimed that France was becoming the new California, 'where the revolver was king'! Rather than remedying structural inequalities, punishment was pursued as the solution. Victor Hugo cut to the heart of the matter when he said, 'There is always more misery among the lower classes than there is humanity in the higher.'"

"Didn't the writings on eugenics of Francis Galton, Charles Darwin's half-cousin, become a useful tool for the ruling class to justify their actions?"

"This was most unfortunate, Olivier. Galton maintained that human character was determined by genes, not education or living conditions. People are bad because they have bad genes. Roman emperor Marcus Aurelius had concluded almost two millennia earlier that poverty was the mother of all crime. To Galton, however, criminality was hereditary."

"Bon-Papa, all these societal changes; urbanization, increases in population and mobility, growing income disparity, evolving expectations and perceptions coupled with a corrupt legal system must have created a great deal of societal pressure and unrest."

"Yes, hence the rise of the Anarchist movement which heightened the already increasing levels of street crime and the court's workload. Ostensibly, this movement was driven by the ideology of rejecting all forms of hierarchy and governmental control. While some were motivated philosophically by this ideology, many followers were drawn in by the stress and desperation caused by injustice, poverty, intolerable working conditions, rising living costs, and low wages. They wanted to destroy a system that had excluded them.

"The rising middle and upper classes obviously felt threatened by this movement. The bourgeoisie believed that the court system did not deal harshly enough with this problem. The lower social classes were thought to be inherently bad, and class warfare ensued. An autocratic agrarian analogy was made that put things into perspective: The lower classes were the sheep, the police were the sheep dogs, and the bourgeois were the shepherds who would fleece the sheep and control the dogs.

"Part of my poem, 'The Flowers of the Embankments,' was inspired by this societal development.

"Il est des gens aussi dont l'âme se mutine
Alors que l'Etat veut les mettre en espalier…,
Qui ont horreur de l'ordre, haïssent la routine,
Le sécateur et le fumier. "

(There are people who are also rebellious,
Although the State wants to control and contain
Those who dislike order, routine, the trellis,
Pruning shears, the muck, the ball and chain.)

"The Spanish philosopher George Santayana's aphorism written in 1905, 'Those who cannot remember the past are condemned to repeat it,' is very well known in my lifetime,

Bon-Papa. Unfortunately, its warning over the past hundred-plus years has not been taken seriously."

"What a shame, Olivier. Santayana was a great admirer of the Roman poet–philosopher Lucretius, as I was. Lucretius's poem 'On the Nature of Things' is such a vitally important and influential work. Lucretius taught how important it is to build on the experiences and knowledge of the past."

I decided I needed another glass of this delicious Burgundy red wine. I subscribe to the theory that wine is enhanced not only by food but also by the locale and the company one keeps. I also like to believe that the wine of a hundred years ago was more authentic and flavorful.

"Olivier, please order one for me as well. After all, since we are being philosophical, wine is bottled philosophy."

I waited until he had a few swallows. The next question was a big one.

"Bon-Papa, how did you respond to the single most defining and destructive legal, political, and societal controversy of your time—the Dreyfus Affair? This was a tragedy that needed to be understood, remembered, and not repeated."

In December 1894, artillery officer Alfred Dreyfus was falsely convicted of treason, which set the stage for one of the worst political crises in French history. It tore the country apart and reverberates to this day.

Captain Dreyfus was accused of selling military secrets to the Germans. He was also Jewish. The Dreyfus affair prompted the anti-Semitism that had been brewing for decades to snowball.

It also revealed a society and government that could be easily manipulated by conspiracy theories of the deceitful and by intimidation.

However, further investigation by some members of the government, newspapers, and the more progressive revealed a massive cover-up.

"I initially believed that the conviction of Alfred Dreyfus was just. *La Croix*, the Roman Catholic newspaper distributed to all parishes, promoted anti-Dreyfus and anti-Semitic propaganda throughout the ordeal. I resisted believing that the military and its allies—the hierarchy of the Church, and the conservative elements of society—could have been so grossly mistaken.

"It was a terrible time. Those who questioned the conviction and were 'pro-Dreyfus' were accused of conspiring against France, the Church, and the military. Families and friendships were torn apart based on individual views of the Dreyfus Affair. The 'pro-Dreyfus' were at risk of being challenged to duels by the 'anti-Dreyfus'—or, perhaps worse, being called 'intellectuals'!"

"Bon-Papa, I have read journalist Émile Zola's scathing denunciation of complicit officials, *J'accuse!* (I Accuse!), which was published in the newspaper *L'Aurore* on January 13, 1898. It was a tipping point in the case."

"Alfred Dreyfus, his family, and the country suffered twelve long years before the conspiracy was thoroughly uncovered.

"While Dreyfus was convicted by a military court, I have no doubt the same result would have occurred in a civil court.

The Dreyfus conviction exposed a malevolent, unhealthy society as well as a corrupt judicial and political system that was subject to personal and hidden agendas not in the best interest of the nation.

"I was appalled by this deliberate miscarriage of justice. When the case completely unraveled and the big lie was laid bare, I was stunned at the undercurrent of deceit and hostility."

"Your poem 'The Snail,' Bon-Papa, reveals your cynicism, frustration, and disgust."

(Au Palais de Justice de Rouen,
le vieux sculpteur a mis sur les feuilles
d'acanthe un escargot symbolique.)

L'ESCARGOT

Cul-de-jatte lourdaud, malfaisant et visqueux
L'escargot salit tout de sa bave argentée;
Promeneur inlassé, dès l'aube il est heureux
De cueillir sur la fleur la tremblante rosée.

Il passe sans remords, calme, majestueux,
Il a souillé la fleur, l'herbe est déshonorée.
Cul-de-jatte lourdaud, malfaisant et visqueux
L'escargot salit tout de sa bave argentée.

Dame Justice, hélas! d'allure est peu pressée;
Elle pose partout son large pied boueux.
Aussi le vieux sculpteur, en sa verve amusée,
A-t-il mis sur nos murs cet emblème fâcheux:
L'escargot, touche-à-tout, malfaisant et visqueux!

(At the Palace of Justice in Rouen,
the old sculptor placed, on the acanthus leaves,
a symbolic snail.)

THE SNAIL

Legless, clumsy, evil, and slimy
The snail, with its silver spittle, dirties everything.
Tireless traveler at dawn, he is happy.
Picking at the dew, he leaves the flowers trembling.

He passes without remorse, calm and stately.
He dishonors the grass, the flowers defiling.
Legless, clumsy, evil, and slimy
The snail, with its silver spittle, dirties everything.

Lady Justice, alas! Not known for her celerity
Plants her large, muddy foot all over.
Therefore, the old sculptor, with amused energy,
Put on our walls this unflattering marker:
The snail touches all, evil and slimy!

Félix Le Molt states that the justice system "touches all … legless, clumsy, evil, and slimy." His analogy comparing a muddy, evil, slimy snail that defiles everything with an essential defining component of society does not engender confidence in the French legal system of his day. This damnation is all the more disturbing coming from an insider.

Apprehensively, the conservative and religious segments of society rationalized that even if Dreyfus were innocent, the consequences of exposing the miscarriage of justice would destroy French society. American historian Henry Adams (1838–1918) reiterated this sentiment: "They can't acquit Dreyfus without condemning France." As such, many people believed it was essential to France's integrity to ignore the truth and keep the lie alive.

Nevertheless, once the truth about the Dreyfus Affair was revealed, it gave rise to a historical and cultural epiphany that profoundly transformed all introspective and justice-minded individuals.

Dreyfus was eventually completely exonerated, reinstated into the army, and served in the First World War. He was even awarded the *Légion d'honneur*, but the injustice and the passions unleashed still haunted the French psyche. This episode exposed virulent European anti-Semitism and tribalism hidden under the thin veneer of propriety, but the worst was yet to come, and the lessons have still not been learned.

On the 100th anniversary of Émile Zola's *J'accuse!* France's Roman Catholic daily paper, *La Croix*, finally apologized for its anti-Semitic editorials during the Dreyfus Affair.

"Olivier, I wrote the poem 'Dogs Barking in the Night' because despite my frustrations and disappointments I recognized the importance of the law, tradition, and order, because the greater evil is anarchy. I was a guardian of society. I had an eternal call of duty. I always strove to do what was right, no matter how dim and hazy the circumstances."

LES CHIENS ABOIENT DANS LA NUIT

On entend s'élever des profondeurs obscures
De la perfide nuit, l'aboi rauque des chiens,
Gardant d'un cœur égal les palais, les masures,
Le toit du prolétaire ou du patricien.

Ecartant les rôdeurs aux troublantes allures,
Sans l'espoir d'un merci, ardent, ne craignant rien,
On entend s'élever des profondeurs obscures
De la perfide nuit, l'aboi rauque des chiens.

Cette voix, menaçant de cruelles morsures
L'envahisseur sournois des logis mitoyens,
C'est la voix de dieu Pan, protecteur des cultures,
C'est l'éternel appel du devoir et du bien
Qu'on entend s'élever des profondeurs obscures.

DOGS BARKING IN THE NIGHT

We hear rising from the depths dim and hazy
The dogs' hoarse bark, in the night perfidious and black,
Protecting with equal passion palaces or shanties,
Homes of proletariat or aristocracy.

Scattering the prowlers menacing and wary
With no need for gratitude, fearless on the attack.
We hear rising from the depths dim and hazy
The dogs' hoarse bark, in the night perfidious and black.

From cruel jaws, that voice threatens and bullies
The sneaky invader entering neighboring sites,

It is the voice of the god Pan, protector of shepherds
    and country,
It is that eternal call of duty and what is right
That we hear rising from depths dim and hazy.

André Gide and the Law

The lives of the author André Gide (1869–1951) and Félix Le Molt (1862–1923) personally and professionally intersected, and they share some compatible philosophical introspection. André Gide provides us with a reinforcing perspective into my great-grandfather's profession.

André Gide won the 1947 Nobel Prize for Literature and is considered one of the dozen top literary giants of the twentieth century. A champion of intellectual honesty, he challenged society to question the values by which it lived. His life, forceful personality, and controversial views on political, social, and sexual matters are to most people now, better known than his literary work.

I pretended to read some of his books in French literature classes, but it wasn't until I discovered Félix Le Molt and his book of poems that I became more closely acquainted with Gide's work.

René Gide, my grandfather and Félix Le Molt's son-in-law, was André Gide's fourth cousin. My grandparents and André Gide traveled in similar literary and artistic circles, which included François Mauriac and André Maurois, though they were not close. The family tree had diverged a century earlier, and they were distanced by religious, political, and moral beliefs.

This familial connection is an interesting sidebar to a larger correlation. Félix Le Molt and André Gide, while close in age and socio-economic status, had very disparate lives. Both men did, however, have strikingly similar opinions about France's justice system. I am not aware that Félix Le Molt ever met André Gide, but their paths may have crossed literally.

André Gide had a fascination for France's judicial system. He kept newspaper articles on the subject, made notations, and followed major legal cases throughout his life. For Gide, the courthouse was one of the four main attractions in a city, along with the municipal park, the marketplace, and the cemetery. Gide often visited a family home in Rouen, and while there sought the responsibilities of being a juror. At age sixty, he collected a summary of these experiences and thoughts and published his book *Judge Not*. The title refers to Christ's Sermon on the Mount, when Jesus admonishes his followers not to rush to judgment and condemn others unfairly: "For by what judgment you judge, you will be judged, and by what measure you measure out, it will be measured to you."

Judge Not, written by an author of acute perception, fortuitously gives us insight into both the judicial process and the social norms my great-grandfather would have worked and lived by. As Félix Le Molt states in his poem "The Snail," the justice system "touches all … legless, clumsy, evil, and slimy," and this is exactly what fascinated André Gide.

André Gide's interest in crime, legality, and consequences has much to do with prevailing social prejudices and inequities, and his penchant for psychology and critiques of societal conventions. Many of his books feature characters with criminal dispositions who are societal misfits, thereby creating an opportunity to initiate philosophical questions.

In Gide's book *The Vatican Cellars (Les caves du Vatican)*, published in 1914, one of the memorable characters, Lafcadio, has no familial bonds, no loyalty to country or society, and is completely amoral, yet navigates life successfully. He commits an *acte gratuit*, a shocking random murder, and suffers no consequences. What accounts for this behavior? Gide wants us to ask. Is there such a thing as a random act? Quoting Goethe, he wrote in his journal, "There are no crimes, however great, that on certain days I have not felt capable of committing."

My great-grandfather acknowledges the existence of this darker or hidden side of human nature in all of us:

LE JARDIN SECRET

Tout homme au fond du cœur a son jardin secret
Où jamais le profane odieux ne pénètre.
Temple charmant. Temple discret
Dont on est soi-même le prêtre.

Sous son triple verrou, mystérieux coffret
Qui ne peut s'entr'ouvrir que sous la main du maître,
Tout homme au fond du cœur a son jardin secret
Où jamais le profane odieux ne pénètre.

Les fruits de ce jardin sont quelquefois mauvais:
Tristes déchets de vie, ou biens legs d'un ancêtre.
La Parque au front ridé veut que son rouet
Le fils rugueux du chanvre au fil d'or s'enchevêtre.
Tout homme au fond du cœur a son jardin secret.

THE SECRET GARDEN

All men in their hearts have their secret garden
Where never can enter an unholy entity.
Sacred temple, temple guarded
Where we are our own authority.

Under triple locks, this mysterious chest, hardened,
Can only be opened by its owner carefully.
All men in their hearts have their secret garden
Where never can enter an unholy entity.

The fruits of this garden are sometimes regrettable:
Ancestral legacy or the sad debris of one's lifetime.
Parca*, with furrowed brow, tries on her trundle
To weave the rough thread of hemp with golden twine.
All men in their hearts have their secret garden.

(*Parca was a goddess in ancient Roman mythology who
directed the lives and deaths of humans. This reference to
Parca, one of the three Fates, might have also been a recognition and appreciation of Paul Valéry's mystical Hellenistic

poem 'La Jeune Parque' published in 1917 and dedicated to André Gide.)

Half of André Gide's book *Judge Not* comprises his experiences as a juror. When he volunteered for jury duty, the court was surprised and hesitant, as this was not an activity normally pursued by members of his social status. Most jurors were selected from the working class; they were predominantly farmers. As a juror, he was circumspect in his questions, not wanting to be removed for being perceived as an "intellectual" who would challenge the proceedings.

While Gide initially opens his book *Judge Not* by complimenting the judges and jurors for being "conscientious," he has strong reservations about the court's fairness and efficacy. Gide points out how intimidating the legal process would be even for him, educated and protected, to face a "kind of throne where three oddly dressed old men sit" in judgment. His observation complements the sentiments expressed in Félix Le Molt's poem, "The Judges."

Gide comments that, given the real and perceived increase in crime during this period, the court tended to show "no mercy." The presumption of guilt was high, and the belief was pervasive that the defendants were guilty of some crime, even if perhaps not the crime before the court. Gide notes how appearance, poor language skills, and a general lack of education revealed by defendants adversely influenced the court. He quotes a question asked by a judge to an uneducated woman with a weather-beaten face who "looked like a charwoman, wearing a short shawl of black wool over a blue apron":

Judge: "What did you do to obviate this disadvantageous deed?"

Woman: ????

This witness never stood a chance to receive a fair hearing.

He did find human justice "doubtful and precarious" and believed that reforms were needed. He concluded that his society lacked the psychological tools to better understand human behavior.

The Swiss psychoanalyst Carl Jung (1875–1961) observed, "Thinking is difficult; that is why most people judge." As a result, society is not protected, nor is justice fairly dispensed. Nevertheless, André Gide took his role as a juror seriously. He took notes and thought through issues; he tried to understand both sides while empathizing with the defendants. The effort left him emotionally drained.

Because my great-grandfather worked in the Rouen Assize Court, he may have been involved with cases André Gide heard as a juror. They may have spoken in the halls. They both arrived, in their own way, at comparable conclusions regarding the judicial process of their time.

Virtue

It was cold and windy. The rain was coming. Bon-Papa and I were not enjoying our walk. The inclement weather conformed to the brewing storm clouds in my heart. Bon-Papa, reciting one of his poems, made this suggestion:

"Ferme ton manteau, voyageur
On entend venir la bourrasque
Qui voudrait t'arracher le cœur
Avec ses griffes de Tarasque.

En rafale tombe la pluie
Dans les vieux nids abandonnés;
Le ciel est barbouillé de suie,
Rentrons chez nous pour tisonner."

(Traveler, close your coat. Hark!
We hear coming the tempest
That wants to rip out your heart
With the claws of Tarasque.

In gusts falls the rain
Into the old empty nests;

The sky is darkened and stained,
Let us go home to seek comfort and rest.)

Back at the house, we sat warming ourselves by the fireplace, with cups of hot chocolate spiked with a shot of Chartreuse. I felt much better prepared to start a conversation on a disconcerting topic.

"Bon-Papa, I am troubled and need your counsel. I know that despite the economic, cultural, and artistic accomplishments France achieved during your lifetime, the country was much divided politically.

"As an American, I am experiencing this situation in my lifetime. There is such polarization that constructive dialog seems impossible. Please give me the benefits of your experience and wisdom."

"First, let us put things into historical context, Olivier. The humiliating defeat of France during the Franco-Prussian War and the very consequential loss of the territory of Alsace-Lorraine created a national feeling of self-doubt, recrimination, and insecurity. This loss of confidence instilled in French society a feeling of national decline, a loss of greatness that left a painful, ever-present scar on the national psyche.

"The inability to achieve a national consensus on how to move forward crippled the country politically. Two distinct, diametrically opposed political alternatives emerged to battle for the hearts and minds of the French people."

"The right and the left. This is what we face, even today."

"Yes. Olivier, interestingly, the political designations of "right" and "left" arose during the French Revolution. Those who supported the king and the status quo sat on the right side of the newly formed National Assembly, while those in favor of change sat on the left."

"Amazing how those literal descriptions have evolved into such hardened permanent political positions."

"During my time, the right was defined as those who believed a return to the monarchy and traditional values was the solution. They had the support of the Church and the military. The right's argument maintained that a partnership between monarchy and Church would provide strong authoritarian leadership and a society with less uncertainty, where the heavy responsibilities of government were entrusted to king and God.

The left was known as the Republicans, and they championed a representative democratic government as well as the progressive agendas of the separation of Church and State and women's rights. The left sought to promote French culture and art, as well as to emphasize the dignity, selfless devotion to country, strength, and wisdom of the common people, thereby promoting democratic traditions that would legitimize the government. They had the support of those who generally preferred a society open to new ideas and the benefits of science."

"So, Bon-Papa, then as now the resulting resentments, distrust, and uncertainties between these competing forces created a state of disequilibrium."

"Voltaire said, 'History never repeats itself; man always does.' Invariably, some people will view difficulties or change as opportunities to self-reflect, propose solutions and work toward an improved future. Conversely, others will want to assign blame. They will promote fear and insecurity and seek a return to the past. In the ensuing struggle, truth and humanity are always casualties."

The epigram by French writer Jean-Baptiste Alphonse in 1849 came to mind:

"*Plus ça change plus c'est la même chose,*" I thought to myself distressingly.

This disturbing dilemma resonated deeply with me, given the current political state of affairs. Throughout history, in response to this tension, social movements are formed that reject information that contradicts cherished beliefs. Alternative facts are sought, truth is displaced, and history is mythologized. The battle lines of us vs. them harden. People resort to what François Mauriac characterizes in his novel *Viper's Tangle* as "a tendency to pick and choose things that nurture our grievances and perpetuate our resentments." A nation in such a situation is in peril.

This realization was troubling. We sat for a while, simply watching the comforting hypnotic flickers of flame. Fire is a source of endless fascination and has a universal magnetic spiritual draw. It satisfies the primeval need for safety and togetherness. It is a reassuring presence.

I took a deep breath and resumed the conversation.

"Please explain, Bon-Papa, the Boulangist political movement."

"In my generation, the reactionary mindset manifested itself with the rise of General Boulanger and the Boulangist Party. This populist movement of various disaffected segments of society—the neglected working class, royalists, traditional Catholics, anti-Semites, and moralists—coalesced into a potent political force. They sought to exact revenge on Germany for France's defeat in the Franco-Prussian war. Adherents also wanted to revise the French constitution and restore the monarchy… to save France, of course.

"General Boulanger was the strong man who would cater to a mythic past and sense of victimhood. There always seem to be people drawn to those who provide superficially decisive leadership with appealingly simplistic solutions to emotionally charged problems.

"Lamentably, Olivier, many people find it far easier to blindly accept lies well told, presented with accompanying deceptive fanfare. These are always more entertaining than the work of facing difficult facts and inconvenient truths.

"The inspirational author and philosopher Anatole France made the following observation: 'That is what the crowd likes; it demands categorical statements and not proofs. Proofs disturb and puzzle it.' He was especially wary of the public's susceptibility to seduction by irrational, fear-mongering demagogues."

"This all sounds so frighteningly familiar Bon-Papa."

"After significant electoral victories by the Boulangist party in January 1889, there was a populist surge toward authoritarianism. General Boulanger became the man who would destroy democracy. The General was encouraged by his supporters to rally the people, create an army, and overthrow the government.

"Boulanger was a symbol to galvanize disparate reactionary and protest voters. However, he was accused of fraud and corruption, and threatened with arrest, whereupon he fled the country. In the September 1889 elections, amidst internal conflicts and contradictions, the Boulangist Party was defeated and dissolved.

"Sometimes we need to follow the actions of the lowly hedgehog. Events move in cycles."

"Please recite your poem on the hedgehog."

"Ce petit sanglier des bois lilliputiens
Quand il sent un danger sur lui-même se roule;
Il peut braver ainsi la morsure des chiens
Et le péril passé, indemne, se déroule.

Il sait que l'océan s'apaise après la houle,
Et qu'après l'ouragan, le ciel devient serein.
Ce petit sanglier des bois lilliputiens
Quand il sent le danger, sur lui-même se roule.

Le sage, aussi, se rit des noirceurs du destin;
Comme le hérisson, il met son cœur en boule,
Disant: «Il fait mauvais…il fera beau demain!»
Il est bon d'imiter, méprisé de la foule,
Le petit sanglier des bois lilliputiens."

(This little boar of the Lilliputian forest
Envelops himself when menace is discerned,
Thereby withstanding the dogs that molest,
Surviving the danger, he is unconcerned.

He knows the ocean subsides after a tempest,
After the storm, clear skies return.
This little boar of the Lilliputian forest
Envelops himself when menace is discerned.

The philosopher also laughs at tribulation;
Like the hedgehog, he protects his heart, saying
"Today is difficult but tomorrow will be outstanding!"
We should imitate him, though he is a vexation,
This little boar of the Lilliputian forest.)

I acknowledged his wisdom with an appreciative nod. Sometimes you have to just ride out the storm.

"As you said Bon-Papa there are patterns in human behavior. The popularity of Boulanger and the nationalist xenophobic authoritarian appeal of Boulangism did not go unnoticed by ambitious and unscrupulous future generations, who realized the potential political opportunities of exploiting fears, prejudices, anger, and greed in a similar manner."

"We must learn from history, Olivier. How we understand the lessons of the past determines who we are. When the laws are not sovereign, there you find demagogues. It is exceedingly dangerous to give an unjust man power. As you observed, unfortunately, Boulanger was soon replaced in my generation by more nefarious characters, such as Maurice Barrès and Léon Daudet among many others."

According to the right, France lost the Franco-Prussian War because of the corruption that foreigners and Jews brought to the country. These xenophobic misinformation campaigns ominously presaged Nazism. A leading proponent of these conspiracy theories was journalist and politician Maurice Barrès (1862–1923). He took the position that France was in moral decay due to rampant socialism, lawlessness, antireligious sentiment, and immigration. He declared, "Foreigners, like a parasite, poison us!" A sensationalist press fed the public these conspiracy theories to explain France's predicament.

Léon Daudet (1867–1942), one of the founders of the right-wing organization *L'Action Française*, wrote that Jews were "goats with human faces, trafficking in gold and dung." Both men and their followers maintained a false belief that malevolent syndicates led by Jews were bent on destroying France from within.

An insidious example of the long-term damaging consequences of these conspiracy theories is the infamous anti-Semitic text published anonymously in 1903, The Protocols of the Elders of Zion. A fabricated hoax, it purported to be the Jewish master plan for world domination. The document quickly circulated across the globe and was promoted as an existential threat by many political and business leaders. Despite resounding evidence of fraud, it was used to indoctrinate German school children on the "Jewish problem." The American industrialist Henry Ford used the Protocols as source material for a series of anti-Semitic articles published in his newspaper. Here was proof that the Jews had a master plan to replace Christianity. Dishearteningly, today we hear accusations of Jewish lasers from space causing havoc, Jewish control of the financial world bankrupting the country, and the chanting "Jews will not replace us" in the streets.

The right, with Church support, further asserted that God disapproved of technological innovations and changing social norms. During funeral services at Notre Dame for those who died during a movie theater fire, the priest attributed the cause of the blaze and subsequent suffering to a manifestation of God's wrath at scientific progress. The ever-contentious Léon Daudet fueled this resentment, blaring, "The Republic does not need any scientists!"

L'Action Française used the politics of xenophobia, divisiveness, and misguided nationalism to stoke the resentment of those who felt culturally unmoored by the changing times and those who had been left behind financially. This cynical manipulation was meant to create a sense of collective victimhood. *L'Action Française* sought to promote that a weak, morally corrupt country was facing existential threats, and that they alone could save it. They wanted to restore the greatness of France, as only they envisioned it had been and should be.

This political organization continued its demagoguery into the 1920s and 1930s, and later blamed the French defeat in World War II on the separation of Church and State, Jews, jazz, loose morals, and so on. They supported the puppet regime of General Pétain and the Vichy government and collaborated with the Nazis, supporting their efforts to resolve "the Jewish problem." They needed the Nazis, of all people, to help them pursue their quest to create a spiritual revival against decadence and moral degeneration. After the war, members would be arrested and convicted of collaborating with the enemy.

"Bon-Papa, how should society respond to such intellectual dishonesty, the grasping for power at any destructive cost, the hypocrisy, the lawlessness of such people and political movements in pursuit of blind ambition and self-aggrandizement?"

"Plato said that the punishment of wise men who refuse to take part in the government is to live under the government of worse men. It is critically important that we properly prepare, educate, and encourage our youth to participate. They must be taught the importance of virtue in civic life. Good citizenship means not only having an appreciation for our rights but also acknowledging our obligation to society. The ancient Romans extolled the concept of virtue—putting the common good before personal interests. We must promote this idea by personal and historic example."

"Putting societal obligations before personal gain. Such a noble approach, Bon-Papa, but are you not concerned that society will not realize and counter impending threats before it is too late?"

"We can draw encouragement that the historic moral development of humanity, while erratic, has in the long run trended towards improvement, Olivier, although it does not happen by itself.

"Ancient Greek and Roman philosophers from Socrates to Aristotle and Seneca encouraged the study of philosophy to increase society's chances of developing competent and wise political leaders. It is a question of building character. The Roman poet Horace used the words *sapere aude*—dare to be wise / dare to do the right thing—to encourage political leaders to be courageous enough to promote and follow the truth and to use reason to pursue the greater good.

"The citizenry must insist that its leaders have virtue. We must take this responsibility. People will get the political leaders they deserve."

"The adage *sapere aude* is certainly not being followed by many political leaders today. They abnegate their responsibilities and violate their oath of office. However, the American founding fathers were men of virtue, Bon-Papa. They avidly studied the writings of ancient Greek and Roman philosophers and created a government of rules, of checks and balances, with the ability to adapt to change. The peaceful transition of presidential power that, until recently, the United States enjoyed for over two hundred years is a testament to their sagacity. While imperfect, they understood the importance of striving to be virtuous in theory and practice, but they had doubts about democracy's ability to withstand corruption and the autocratic tendencies of segments of society."

"Managing this conflict is a perennial challenge faced by every generation, Olivier. In every society, there are factions attracted to authoritarianism from a combination of fear, hate, greed, and lust for power. We must continually reconcile philosophical morality with the realities of power and politics. We must not overreact; power must be exercised with principle as the cure cannot be worse than the disease, and yet we must constantly be vigilant and realize that this struggle is never-ending. Friedrich Nietzsche warned, 'In individuals, insanity is rare: but in groups, parties, nations, and epochs, it is the rule.'"

"I see, Bon-Papa, that you were concerned about lies and malicious conspiracy theories put forth by duplicitous individuals and corrupt institutions. In your poem, 'The Flowers of the Embankments,' you encourage the reader to:

Research justice, without prejudice,
Scorn the schemer, he is wanton,
Fear favoritism as much as injustice,
Bend in a storm and then straighten."

"Olivier, I will again quote Marcus Aurelius: 'There is but one thing of real value—to cultivate truth and justice, and to live without anger in the midst of lying and unjust men.' A lifelong quest for knowledge and the application of acquired wisdom are essential tools that can help us understand our world and ourselves; these can prevent us from being led astray by the unprincipled."

"Thank you, Bon-Papa."

The beginnings of the twentieth century were tempest-tossed, with horrific storm clouds on the horizon. Unfortunately, the social and political establishments of many countries were unable to contain the false demonization that appealed to fear and prejudice, remedy social injustice, combat zealous nationalism, and resist rising authoritarianism. There would be tragic consequences.

The upheavals my great-grandfather's world experienced have striking and potentially dangerous parallels today. I wonder how future historians will complete the following sentence: *The beginnings of the twenty-first century were tempest-tossed …*

War

The social, technological, and scientific advances of *La Belle Époque* had a darker side—a corresponding effect on military technology. European nations competed in an arms race, and militarization was as rampant as it is today. This led to significant international tensions and proxy wars. It was inevitable that military technology would be used to settle old scores. This realization contributed to the era's giddiness in some and unease in others. Gaiety coexisted with a sense of foreboding—a pattern that is evident throughout twentieth-century history. The outbreak of World War I was initially viewed as a long-overdue catharsis that would clear the air. No one could have imagined the tragedy that would follow.

Bon-Papa and I were walking through a rolling field on the outskirts of Bourbonne-les-Bains. We were engulfed and intoxicated by the blanket of bright wildflowers, the blue sky, and the warm sun. It was the epitome of rural peace and beauty.

I tried to imagine how many such flourishing fields were transformed by the Great War into wastelands of unspeakable horror. Fields filled with mutilated bodies, scarred by barbed wire and bomb craters, and ravaged by rat-infested trenches seemed so far removed from this idyllic setting. The battle site of Verdun, where casualties exceeded 750,000, was only 100 miles away.

"Bon-Papa, having experienced Le Chat Noir with you, I have a better understanding of your poem 'Hallucination,' but it is still complex. Could you explain it?"

HALLUCINATION

Les hauts arbres du parc, la nuit, sur le ciel sombre
Ressemblent aux décors découpés du «Chat Noir»
Alors qu'on y faisait de l'or avec de l'ombre
Et que Salis était seigneur de ce manoir.

La lune qui paraît brusquement nous fait voir,
Galopant, d'Iéna, les cavaliers sans nombre;
Les hauts arbres du parc, la nuit, sur le ciel sombre
Ressemblent aux décors découpés du «Chat Noir».

Puis la lune s'en va, emportant la pénombre
Et la nuit sur le ciel abat son éteignoir.
L'histoire a sa magie, les faits qu'elle dénombre
Se reflètent parfois dans l'antique miroir
Des grands arbres du parc, la nuit, sur le ciel sombre.

Versailles 1911

HALLUCINATION

The tall trees of the park, in the dark sky, at night,
Resemble the cutout shapes of the "Chat Noir"

While we made gold without sunlight
And Salis was lord of this manor.

The moon appearing suddenly brings the sight
Galloping, from Jena, horsemen without number.
The tall trees of the park, in the dark sky, at night,
Resemble the cutout shapes of the "Chat Noir."

The moon then departs, taking the twilight,
And the night sky becomes obscure.
History has its magic, the facts it recites
Are sometimes reflected in the antique mirror
Of the tall trees of the park, in the dark sky, at night.

Versailles 1911

"There are several different thoughts and emotions here. I am trying to sort and respond to a tangle of thoughts and concerns. First, please note that I wrote this at Versailles, and Napoleon plays a prominent role."

"You resurrect the image of two historical figures revered in French society: Louis XIV and Napoleon. Both men represented national greatness."

"Yes, the perception of past and lost national greatness. In 1806, Napoleon led France in the Battle of Jena against Frederick of Prussia. It was a decisive victory for man and country. Ten days later, after defeating the Prussians further, Napoleon entered Berlin in triumph."

"Your focus, Bon-Papa, on this glorious military success over the Germans from a century earlier only underscores the prevailing defeatism in France during your time. The poem illustrates the zeitgeist of a time when people would focus on past national successes to mollify their present insecurities."

"Absolutely. This is reinforced by the intentional juxtaposition of this past military victory, glorified in the *L'Épopée* show we saw, and with overall happenings at *Le Chat Noir*, where the populace could be distracted by the newly created entertainments of modernity in a reassuring environment.

"Sadly, despite the jollity at *Le Chat Noir*, there existed throughout society a simmering, disturbing fascination that another war with Germany would be necessary, and even justified, to restore honor to France. Schools were permeated by a fervent nationalism that promoted to students the patriotic duty of becoming soldiers and making sacrifices for the glory of France. The demons of humiliation needed to be exorcized."

"Does the title 'Hallucination' imply that this war fervor and its objectives were based on false notions and beliefs and are delusional visions of national grandeur?"

"The last stanza gives us the 'morality.' The bright moon that illuminated the great success at Jena has now departed and leaves us in the dark, but our history lives within us. The past is interwoven with the present. We see ourselves in the distant mirror of the past.

"The horsemen would soon be riding again, Olivier."

Bon-Papa did not want to speak any further of the Great War.

La Belle Époque ended with the shattering slaughter of World War I. Approximately 1.4 million French were killed, and millions more were wounded and rendered invalids. It was a pyrrhic victory for France—which technically won and could therefore impose humiliating terms on Germany, including the return of Alsace-Lorraine. France, however, was bled white by the conflict and couldn't withstand the German blitzkrieg in Round Three. Despite the devastation, World War I would pale in comparison to what would happen twenty years later.

Félix Le Molt's poetry makes only one obvious reference to this catastrophic event. His poem "The Cut Hay," written at the start of the conflict, projects an exalted tone of worthy sacrifice, honor, and glory. The ultimate cost and human tragedy must have been a tremendous shock to him.

LE FOIN COUPÉ

L'herbe n'a de parfum que lorsqu'elle est fanée
Et meurt dans les grands clos, à l'ombre des pommiers,
Lorsque la faux courbant sa tête profanée
A coups rythmés la couche au travers des sentiers.

Forêt qui n'a vécu que pendant une année,
Où l'insecte farouche a traqué son gibier,
L'herbe n'a de parfum que lorsqu'elle est fanée
Et meurt dans les grands clos, à l'ombre des pommiers.

O vous, obscurs soldats de la lutte acharnée
Herbe du champ français que va trancher l'acier,
De nos succès prochains, rançon prédestinée,
Songez, quand vous tombez en cueillant vos lauriers,
Que l'herbe n'a d'odeur que lorsqu'elle est fanée!

Rouen 1914

THE CUT HAY

Grass only has scent after the cutting,
As it dies under shady apple trees, in great mounds,
When the scythe, its profane head bending
In rhythmic strokes cuts it down.

A forest that was only a yearling,
Where their prey the wild insects would hound,
Grass only has scent after the cutting
As it dies under shady apple trees, in great mounds.

You are unknown soldiers in relentless endeavor,
Cut down by steel, the grass of French territory
For our future success, a predetermined expenditure.
Know, when you fall while earning your glory,
That grass only has scent after the cutting!

Rouen 1914

Philippe Le Molt, my great-grandfather's son, for reasons lost in the mists of family history, did not serve as a soldier in the Great War, but his cousin Michel de Bellomayre did. Michel never got to have adventures riding the American prairies with his friends and Buffalo Bill. Instead, he suffered the experience of modern combat. Given the heavy casualties France suffered and the desperate need for manpower, Michel was conscripted as a mature man of thirty-seven to fight in the trenches. He wrote the following heart-wrenching visceral poems, as the horrors enfolded him:

PARIS (EXTRAIT)

Boueux, fourbus, vêtus de capotes souillées,
Traînant à pas pesants nos hardes épouillées
Dont la glaise et le sang maculaient le bleu clair,
Après six mois de front nous venions de l'enfer...

Juin 1918

PARIS (EXCERPT)

Muddy, tired, wearing our soiled caps,
Dragging with heavy steps our tattered packs
The pale blue stained by blood and clay,
After six months at the front we return from hell in disarray...

June 1918

LETTRE AVANT L'ASSAUT (EXTRAIT)

Un mois plus tard.
Front de Champagne, Perthes-les-Hurlus

Juillet 1918

Adieu! Je suis élu pour le grand sacrifice...
L'heure approche... ma vie est comme un édifice
Sous lequel le sol tremble et qui va s'écouler;
Tout le décor terrestre à l'air de chanceler;

. . . .

Voici l'heure d'entrer dans mon éternité;
Je suis vêtu déjà d'un linceul de clarté;
Nos lignes sont en flamme et la tranchée explose;
Mais, en allant vers Dieu, je crierai quelque chose
Parmi l'alléluia triomphal du canon:
Ce soir, je vais mourir en redisant ton nom...

LETTER BEFORE THE ASSAULT (EXCERPT)

One month later

Front de Champagne. Perthes-les-Hurlus

July 1918

Goodbye! I have been chosen for the great sacrifice…
The hour approaches… my life is like an edifice
Under which the ground trembles and crumbles;
All the earth around us disassembles;

. . . .

My time has come to enter eternity;
I am already clothed in a shroud of clarity;
Our lines are enflamed and the trench explodes;
But, moving toward God, I will shout this ode….
Amongst the cannon's triumphal halleluiah I exclaim:
Tonight, I will die while once more saying your name…

My distant cousin delayed his "rendezvous with Death" and survived this horrendous ordeal. After the war, he reunited with his family, became a successful lawyer, and left us his voice in the form of several poetry books. He was awarded the prestigious Prix Paul Verlaine in 1942 by *L'Académie française* for his book *La Tragédie Humaine* (*The Human Tragedy*). I recently acquired an autographed copy dated October 29, 1946. I run my finger over his signature, and I look forward to our conversations.

To most French people during *La Belle Époque*, their world seemed in continual crisis. Not very *belle* at all. It is ironic, therefore, that this period of French history between the

Franco-Prussian War and World War I was eventually dubbed "The Golden Age." The rationale was that despite uncertainty, unprecedented social change, and political chaos, there had been phenomenal economic growth and peace for forty-three years, and France had once again ascended to cultural world leadership.

Given the turmoil of the following twenty-five years, people would look back with fondness at *La Belle Époque*. After the nightmare of World War I came the Spanish flu, which killed over 200,000 French citizens and an estimated 50 million worldwide. The "Roaring 20s," as it was known in the United States, quickly disintegrated into the worldwide Great Depression, and that ushered in a new era with its own frightening changes and seemingly insurmountable problems. The cataclysm of World War II was just around the corner. Poet and philosopher Paul Valéry interprets the mood of the 1930s with his observation, "The trouble with our times is that the future is not what it used to be."

The Flowers of the Embankments

I have frequently referred to Félix Le Molt's poem *"Les fleurs des talus"* ("The Flowers of the Embankments"), as it is a telling declaration and reveals the evolution of his thought. Written at his country house in Bourbonne, the village where he was born, and dated a few years before his death, the poem could well be one of his last literary efforts. It is thoughtful and deliberate; it demonstrates his ability to observe and admire while seeking to understand and disseminate moralities. He projects a life well examined.

"The Flowers of the Embankments," Le Molt's longest poem, adopts a different poetic structure from his others to deliver its allegorical message and reveal a personal conflict. This poem makes clear his distaste for the dogmatic, the mundane, and the controlled; it also reveals his envy and admiration for the rebellious, the risky, and the adventurous—those who choose to live "on the edge." As a distinguished magistrate, an upholder of the societal status quo, he must have felt that he did not have the luxury of choosing an untrodden path.

The poem begins by evoking the pastoral and botanical themes of a Claude Monet painting beloved for its ability to impart the mystical impression and quintessential beauty of the French countryside. The tone then shifts abruptly with a satirical compliment to the heavily controlled and structured gardens of the city. These plants, although bountiful and beautiful, are captives and, in comparison to their country cousins, are simply pale effigies "without personality." Some seek to break free from their oppression. Their seeds are released into the wind.

In "The Flowers of the Embankments," Le Molt details the abundance of botanical diversity when nature is left in its natural, unfettered state. Through this analogy, he encourages us to break free from the conventional norms of society and to strive to live deliberately.

Félix Le Molt celebrates this idea in the following excerpt from "The Flowers of the Embankments."

C'est la Thébaïde accueillante
Aux songes sans fin des rêveurs,
L'asile où la vie est calmante
Loin des plaisirs et des honneurs.
La poésie et la musique,
Le cher livre trop vite lu
Voilà toute la politique
Gouvernant l'homme des talus!

It is a Thebaid inviting,
With dreams without end for dreamers
An asylum, where life is soothing
Far from honors and pleasures.
Music and poetry
The cherished book too quickly read
There is all the polity
Governing men on the edge!

"The Flowers of the Embankments" ends with an *envoi*, a message, from the poet to his readers to clarify, embellish, and enhance the poem. He seeks to impart wisdom learned and allow others to build upon it. As Félix Le Molt composed this poem and its envoi at the end of his life and his distinguished career, he reflected on the challenges he faced and the choices he made, on what is important in life and what makes life worth living.

He begins by advising us that no matter how life has positioned us, it is our duty to figure out a way to be content. In his envoi, Félix Le Molt summarizes time-honored philosophical coping techniques. He recommends having a solid moral core with emotional flexibility, philosophically adopting a long-term view, avoiding highs and lows, remaining close to nature, being bold and dreaming, but remaining realistic and practical. Ultimately, he concludes that cultivating wisdom, morality, courage, and moderation are the keystones to finding happiness.

The envoi ends with the unambiguous endorsement, "Choose your place at the edge of life." His message is for each of us to live our own lives fully and become who we really are.

This imagery brings to mind Nietzsche's treacherous hiking escapades in the Swiss Alps. Pushing himself to the edges of mountainous cliffs, Nietzsche developed his concept of the *Übermensch*, or "Overman," an approach to life that both terrifies and inspires: challenge yourself, do not accept mediocrity, reject decadent shallowness, climb higher, and be better by making your own choices.

With his accumulation of both personal and professional experiences, my great-grandfather projects confidence in the future and recommends personal exploration: "[T]ake flight from the dull earth." Break free, branch out, be broad-minded, pursue curiosity and imagination, and remain awed. This is preferable to the alternative of becoming jaded, adopting simple solutions, and taking a seemingly safer approach to life.

Félix Le Molt understands the importance of cultivating flexible thought. He acquires the ability to absorb contradictions and evolve. He makes the conscious decision to acknowledge that the human condition is imperfect, yet he chooses to look beyond it. He dedicates himself to being a man of letters, a *réfléchisseur*, a thinker. He understands the importance, as *La Belle Époque* author and poet Rainer Maria Rilke (1875–1926) would later put it, of living the questions now.

Félix Le Molt believed that it is best to embrace rather than resist uncertainty and ambiguity to find tranquility and achieve equanimity. We can make conscious choices to guide us in how best to live. After a thoughtful life well lived, Félix Le Molt, my great-grandfather, invites us to live a fully realized life… and to cultivate a smile like Candide.

Despite Le Molt's many religious poems written throughout his life, this possibly final poem does not suggest that religious beliefs are a source of enlightenment. There is no hint of seeking divine intervention. We create our meaning in life by the choices we make. My great-grandfather, in the final analysis, believed that, as rational individuals, the responsibility to shape our lives is ours and ours alone.

ENVOI

De quelque façon qu'on te nomme,
Ou cardinal, ou prince, ou gueux,
Puisque tu n'es jamais qu'un homme
Il te faudra pour être heureux
Rechercher l'équité, jamais le bénéfice,
Mépriser l'intrigant et le laisser passer,
Redouter la faveur autant que l'injustice,
Te courber sous l'orage et puis te redresser,
Eviter l'optimisme et la mélancolie,
Admirer le soir sombre et le matin vermeil,
Te choisir une place au talus de la vie
Les pieds dans les cailloux, mais la tête au soleil!

Bourbonne, Septembre 1920

ENVOI

However you are chosen
A cardinal, prince, or mendicant,

Since you are never more than a person,
Find your own way to be content.
Research justice, without prejudice,
Scorn the schemer, he is wanton,
Fear favoritism as much as injustice,
Bend in a storm and then straighten,
Avoid excess optimism, sadness, and strife,
Admire the quiet evening and morning vermilion,
Choose your place at the edge of life,
With feet on the ground but head in the heavens!

Bourbonne, September 1920

It is unfortunate that Félix Le Molt did not leave us additional books of poetry or prose. Literature enables us to access the minds of others and channel the history of ideas. This experience plants a seed, a seed that can repeatedly germinate in the present and set in motion a journey of discovery. The reader of such literature is empowered to participate and is given the opportunity to harvest this past, enrich the present, reflect, and seed the future. It is through words, written words carefully preserved, that we enticingly find connection and build upon the knowledge and wisdom of past generations. The Roman poet Horace informs us, *Littera scripta manet*—the written word remains.

Over the past ten years, I have enjoyed reading and rereading the poetry of my great-grandfather. His book of poems initiated a conversation; his expression of human creativity, reason, and imagination was the catalyst.

My interpretations of these poems may have expanded their original intent, but such is the extraordinary regenerating power of art. "To understand a masterpiece is to recreate it in oneself over again," wrote Anatole France. Through reliving his life by becoming immersed in his private thoughts and putting myself into his time and place, I embraced Félix Le Molt as an integral part of my life, with a special intimacy heightened by his obscurity. When I read his poems, I felt that he was speaking to me alone. I consider myself most fortunate that the looms of fate chose to weave our lives together.

"*Mon cher petit-fils*, I will now ask you a question. You have lived, thus far, a decade longer than I did. Have you done an assessment of your life? Did you learn how best to practice the art of living?"

"Well, cher Bon-Papa, to quote Michelangelo at age 83, 'I am still learning'.

"You have been a role model for me. In the process of reawakening your voice, I found another. Your poetry gave me the motivation to learn more about poetry and to strive to create my poems and improve myself. While I will never be a true poet, the experience has been rewarding. I admit to emulating your use of the rondeau form and attempting to imitate you. As an homage, I wrote the following poem and then, as a twist, translated it into French for you! I hope you will approve and adjudicate my efforts favorably."

"Bravo, Olivier! And thank you for thinking of me."

BIRDS IN EARLY MORNING

The birds in early morning meet and greet
So full of life, they gather and chatter.
Full day ahead, many tasks to complete,
A world to explore, promise and danger.

In harmonious song and sound, they speak,
At length, plans in hand, they quickly scatter.
The birds in early morning meet and greet,
So full of life, they gather and chatter.

The journey of life, grandeur and deceit,
Joys, woes; ephemeral yet eternal,
These moments… memories to share and keep,
Cherish the innocence, and promise vernal,
Of birds, in early morning, who meet and greet.

Magnolia porch, May 2019

LES OISEAUX AU PETIT MATIN

Les oiseaux au petit matin viennent se rencontrer
Débordant de vie, ils se réunissent et babillent.
Une journée pleine de tâches à compléter,
Un monde à découvrir, promesses et périls.

En chants harmonieux il faut bavarder,
Enfin, projets en mains, rapidement ils s'envolent.
Les oiseaux au petit matin viennent se rencontrer
Débordant de vie, ils se réunissent et babillent.

La vie qui passe, avec ses gloires et ses revers,
Ses joies et ses malheurs; éphémères mais éternels,

Ces moments… souvenirs à garder et à partager,
Chérissons l'innocence et la promesse vernale,
Des oiseaux, au petit matin, qui viennent se rencontrer.
Porche de Magnolia, Mai 2019

Guided by the wisdom of my ancestor and his developed philosophy of life, I discovered that his voice encourages us to:

Remember the past—be a student of history, appreciate, learn from, and build upon the lessons it contains, respect the rule of law.

Live in the present—Cultivate happiness, maintain wonder and creativity, enjoy family and friends.

Fear not the future—question, accept, and adapt to change, maintain and encourage virtue, dream but be realistic.

These lessons have been passed down over time, forging a chain, as Bon-Papa wrote in *Le vieux secrétaire*, "guiding our scions, along their uncertain terrain." A bond was created across generations, and the conversation continues.

Acknowledgements

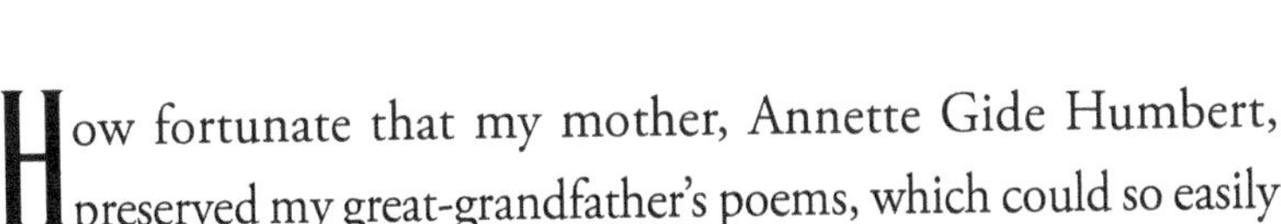

How fortunate that my mother, Annette Gide Humbert, preserved my great-grandfather's poems, which could so easily have been lost. Her invaluable gift was transformational for me.

I am thankful to Dominique Clément from the French Cultural Center / Alliance Française of Boston and Patricia Peknik, author and professor, for their knowledgeable interpretive analysis of my great-grandfather's poetry.

A special thank you to Daphné Allanore de Baritault for her kind and much-needed review of my French orthography. I remain solely responsible for any errors.

My gratitude to Wendy Goldman-Rohm of the Rohm Literary Agency for her advice, which helped sharpen my focus.

Special recognition is due to my sister Nathalie for her insightful details and indispensable knowledge of family history, and to my brother Xavier for the guidance he has always generously given.

I wish to express profound appreciation to my wife and muse Susan for providing the spark that ignited the passion essential to writing this book. With love, wisdom, and encouragement, she made the book and me better.

Genealogical Charts

LE MOLT ANCESTRAL CHART

Phillip Alexander Le Molt (judge, 1765–1845)

|

Félix Le Molt (physician, 1798–1843)

|

Alexander Le Molt (lawyer, 1821–1891)

|

Félix Le Molt (judge, 1862–1923)

My third great-grandfather (my great-grandfather's grandfather) also had the name Félix Le Molt. The elder Félix wrote a thirty-page essay on the history, characteristics, and merits of the thermal springs at Bourbonne—*Notice sur Bourbonne et ses eaux thermals*. The book is considered a historical document and is available to purchase online.

GIDE ANCESTRAL CHART

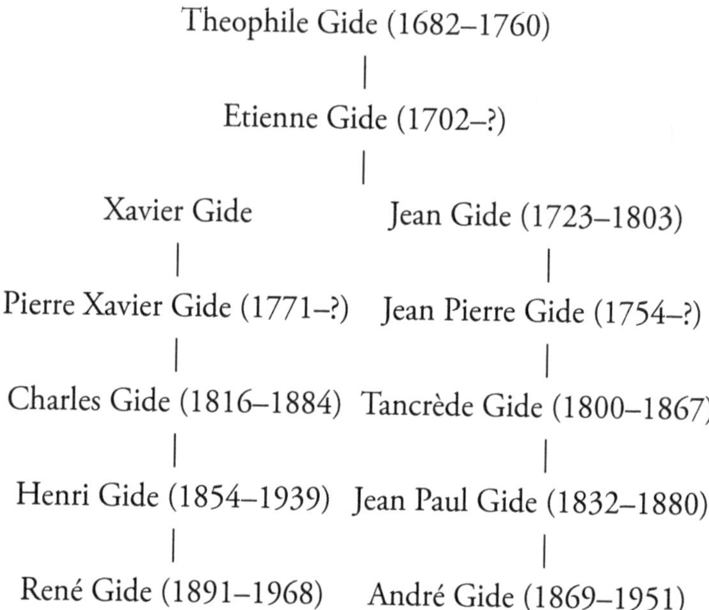

René Gide, my grandfather and Félix Le Molt's son-in-law, was André Gide's fourth cousin. André Gide was the 1947 Nobel Prize laureate in literature.

La Vie Qui Passe

Poems With Translations

PRÉFACE

Comme des champignons quelque peu vénéneux,
Ces rondeaux ont poussé sous bois, dans la fougère,
Dans la calme forêt, aux bruits mystérieux,
Où le bonheur est grand et la peine légère.

Parfois, on les lisait le soir, à la lumière,
Et puis, le lendemain, on ne parlait plus d'eux.
Comme des champignons quelque peu vénéneux,
Ces rondeaux ont poussé sous bois, dans la fougère.

Pourquoi vont-ils sortir de leur sommeil heureux?
Mieux valait un tiroir pour demeure dernière.
Ils n'ont rien à gagner d'un jour trop lumineux;
Je crains que leur lecture, hélas! Ne se digère
Comme des champignons quelque peu vénéneux.
Rouen 1922

PREFACE

Like mushrooms that are somewhat poisonous,
These verses grew among ferns, under wood,
In the calm forest with noises mysterious,
Where trouble is gentle, and there is much good.

Sometimes, they were read by lamp light luminous,
And then next morning forgotten for good,
Like mushrooms that are somewhat poisonous,
These verses grew among ferns, under wood.

Why should they awaken from their happy night?
In the back of a drawer, it is better to stay.
They have nothing to gain from the sunlight;
That their message not be digested, I pray
Like mushrooms somewhat poisonous.
Rouen 1922

I

LES VISIONS

VISIONS

LES YEUX

Les yeux, ces deux jumeaux, embrassent l'infini
Sans jamais pouvoir se connaître.
Ces miroirs d'un émail bleu, noir, ou bien jauni,
De notre âme sont la fenêtre.

S'ignorant, séparés, bien que toujours unis
Pour ouvrir le monde à leur maître,
Les yeux, ces deux jumeaux, embrassent l'infini
Sans jamais pouvoir se connaître.

Par la lune dormant sur les flots aplanis,
Par l'aurore qui vient de naître,
Par le printemps, tout fier des soleils rajeunis,
Par les larmes surtout…peut-être,
Les yeux, ces deux jumeaux, embrassent l'infini.

THE EYES

The eyes, these two twins, embrace the eternal,
Never possibly knowing one another.
These enameled mirrors: black, yellow, beryl,
The windows to our souls they uncover.

Unaware, separate yet always mutual,
They open the world to their master.
The eyes, these two twins, embrace the eternal,
Never possibly knowing one another.

By the quiet moon, on calm waves,
By the dawn reborn,
By the springtime, proud of its young rays,
By the tears especially . . . forlorn.
The eyes, these two twins, embrace the eternal.

LA PÂLE LUMIÈRE DU COLCHIQUE

Sur les prés le colchique allume sa veilleuse
Alors que le soleil s'éteint à l'horizon;
Etrange feu follet sur l'écharpe onduleuse
De la nuit, qui s'en vient surprendre les gazons.

Messager annonçant la saison rigoureuse,
Frêle enfant de l'automne à la fauve toison,
Sur les prés le colchique allume sa veilleuse
Alors que le soleil s'éteint à l'horizon.

Sous le voile trompeur d'une grâce charmeuse,
Sa mortelle beauté enfante le poison;
Le soir, pour embellir sa tige vénéneuse,
Portant avec orgueil de mauves floraisons,
Sur les prés le colchique allume sa veilleuse.
Bourbonne

THE PALE LIGHT OF THE CROCUS

In the meadow the crocuses alight
While the sun descends on its ambit voyage;
On rolling hills strange will-o'-wisps in sight
Startling the grasses and tillage.

Heralding the upcoming season's plight,
Autumn's frail child of saffron pelage,
In the meadow the crocuses alight
While the sun descends on its ambit voyage.

With false premise and abundant charm,
Within her fateful beauty, toxicity abides;
At night, to embellish its stem of harm,
Violet flowers displayed with pride,
In the meadow the crocuses alight.
Bourbonne

ENTRE PARIS ET ROUEN, LA NUIT
PAR LA PORTIERE DU WAGON

Au sein mystérieux des plaines endormies
S'allument, une à une, en des obscurs lointains
Les lampes des hameaux, étoiles assoupies
Qui contemplent le ciel d'un regard incertain.

Lampes, vous attestez que subsiste la vie,
Qu'il reste encore du feu dans l'âtre qui s'éteint.
Au sein mystérieux des plaines endormies
Vous piquez vos clous d'or dans des obscurs lointains.

Mais voilà que la lune, au ras des saules, brille,
Et la Seine revêt sa cuirasse d'étain;
Par les monts et les bois, étrange Walkyrie,
Poursuivant dans la nuit son éternel destin
Au sein mystérieux des plaines endormies.

BETWEEN PARIS AND ROUEN, NIGHT
THROUGH THE TRAIN CAR WINDOW

All across the mysteriously sleeping prairie,
Alight, one by one, in the obscure distance,
The lights of the hamlets, as stars drowsy
That contemplate the sky with hesitance.

Glowing lights, you confirm life's vitality.
The dying hearth fires confirm its existence.
All across the mysteriously sleeping prairie,
Your golden nails pierce through the distance.

But now the moon against the willows shines,
And the Seine dons its armor silvery.
Through the hills and woods, a strange Valkyrie,
Pursuing in the night its eternal destiny,
All across the mysteriously sleeping prairie.

VERSAILLES

Dans la brume du soir, au bas de la terrasse,
Louis regarde, l'œil las, l'autre soleil mourir.
Le roi devine au poids dont les ans le terrassent
Que finit le chemin qu'il devait parcourir.

Songeant à l'enfant-roi dont l'ère va s'ouvrir,
Sombre lui apparaît l'avenir de sa race...
Dans la brume du soir, au bas de la terrasse,
Louis regarde, l'œil las, l'autre soleil mourir.

Ce pouvoir qu'établit sa volonté tenace
Entre de faibles mains ne va-t-il pas périr?
C'est pourquoi le grand roi pressent une menace
Dans la fin du soleil qui vient de s'évanouir
Dans la brume du soir, au bas de la terrasse.
Automne 1911

VERSAILLES

In the twilight of night, at the end of the terrace,
Louis, wearily, observes the other sun's decay.
The king feels the crushing weight of agedness
That will end the role he had to play.

Thinking of the child king and his coming fray
He feels a darkness descend upon his race...
In the twilight of night, at the end of the terrace
Louis, wearily, observes the other sun's decay.

This power of tenacious determination
Will it not perish with vulnerability?
It is why the great king feels a premonition
In the dying sun, with its fragility,
In the twilight of night, at the end of the terrace.
Autumn 1911

VISION CRÉPUSCULAIRE

Dans un ciel embrasé meurt le soleil couchant
Générateur fécond des gloires flamboyantes;
Au ras de l'horizon, l'ombre en s'épaississant
Evoque de la nuit les heures effrayantes.

D'un inlassable effort, la mer, tout doucement,
Roule le lourd feston de ses vagues mourantes.
Dans un ciel embrasé meurt le soleil couchant
Générateur fécond des gloires flamboyantes.

D'horreur semble figé le long cheminement
Des rochers, alourdis par leurs herbes gluantes;
Et le reflet du soir, en son miroitement
Donne un aspect de neige aux tristes eaux dormantes.
Dans un ciel embrasé meurt le soleil couchant.

Jetée de Saint-Valery 1919

A TWILIGHT VISION

The setting sun dies within a blazing heaven,
Bountiful creator of glorious brightness.
At the horizon's edge, shadows thicken
Evoking the fearful hours of the darkness.

The sea, with tireless effort, soft and silken
Rolls the heavy chain of its dying waves.
The setting sun dies within a blazing heaven
Bountiful creator of glorious brightness.

In frozen horror along the coastline
The rocks weighted by the clinging grasses;
And the glint of night with its shine
Create the illusion of snow on the sleeping waves.
The setting sun dies within a blazing heaven.

Jetty of Saint-Valery 1919

L'AUTOMNE

Voilà l'automne qui s'avance
Semant de l'or sur les coteaux;
Il a le calme et l'opulence
Des trois mages orientaux
Qui suivaient l'étoile en silence
Pour voir Jésus dans son berceau…
Voilà l'automne qui s'avance
Semant de l'or sur les coteaux.

La caille a fui vers la Provence
La vieille, au bois, fait des fagots,
Sur l'aire sèche la semence,
Le berger rentre son troupeau,
Voilà l'automne qui s'avance!…

Bourbonne 1913

AUTUMN

Autumn makes its entrance
Sowing gold on the hill's gradient.
He has the calm and opulence
Of the three kings of the Orient
Who followed the star in silence
To see Jesus in his cradle, radiant.
Autumn makes its entrance
Sowing gold on the hill's gradient.

The quail, towards Provence have flown,
The old woman makes her wooden stacks,
The seeds dry air-blown.
The shepherd returns with his pack.
Autumn makes its entrance!

Bourbonne 1913

MIRAGE

Ombrageant l'eau qui dort, de vieux arbres, géants
Immuables et droits se dressent vers les nues;
Leurs fûts, vêtus de gui méprisent l'ouragan;
Seul, on voit, près des nids, la feuille qui remue.

Quand ils vont se mirer, ces arbres, dans l'étang
Leurs troncs ne forment plus que lignes saugrenues.
Tout le long du canal, de vieux arbres, géants
Immuables et droits se dressent vers les nues.

C'est par ses propres yeux qu'on doit juger les gens:
Le reflet de la glace augmente ou atténue;
Tout miroir est doué d'un pouvoir déformant
Ne nous laissons pas prendre à la ligne imprévue
Qui présentent dans l'eau les vieux arbres géants.
Versailles

MIRAGE

The old giant trees shading the sleeping water
Immutable and upright, reach up toward the skies;
Their trunks, draped in mistletoe, despise the thunder;
Near the birds' nests, a leaf's movement catches our eye.

The reflection of these trees in the pond
Reveal their trunks in ludicrous guise.
The old giant trees along the canal becalmed,
Immutable and upright, reach up toward the skies.

Only from one's own eyes can we judge the other.
The reflection of the glass may deflate or augment.
All mirrors are gifted with the ability to alter.
Let us not take the incorrect sentiment
That the old giant trees reflect on the water.
Versailles

LA LUMIÈRE SOUS BOIS

La lumière est douce et sa face est sereine
Sous les bois on la voit s'avancer à pas lents;
Elle met un sourire à l'écorce du chêne,
Et la fougère mâle a des reflets d'argent.

Tout le long des sentiers, l'ombre en tremblant se traîne
Et par les chemins creux se faufile en rampant.
La lumière est douce et sa face est sereine
Sous les bois on la voit s'avancer à pas lents.

Dans les rais de soleil, fantasque et incertaine
La mouche aux ailes d'or s'élance en bourdonnant.
Apre sur les coteaux, cruelle dans la plaine,
Sous les halliers discrets aux tapis odorants
La lumière est douce et sa face est sereine.

THE LIGHT IN THE FOREST

The light is soft and its face serene,
Through the woods, we see its slow progression:
On the oak's bark, a smile beams,
The ferns show a silvery reflection.

Down the path, the trembling shadows careen
And by the sunken trails leave their impression.
The light is soft and its face serene,
Through the woods, we see its slow progression.

In the sun's rays, fanciful and wavering,
The fly with golden wings bombilates and plays.
Harsh on the hills, on the plains unrelenting,
But under hidden thickets, with fragrant baize,
The light is soft, and its face serene.

REFLETS SUR L'EAU

Sur l'eau que l'enfant tient dans le creux de sa main
L'immensité des cieux, au soleil se reflète;
Illusion, sans doute, et trésor incertain,
Mais sur terre, où trouver félicité parfaite!

L'enfant ouvre les doigts, préparant son chagrin
Et tout l'azur s'enfuit dans une gouttelette!
Sur l'eau que l'enfant tient dans le creux de sa main
L'immensité des cieux, au soleil se reflète.

Le bonheur n'est jamais, au fond du cœur humain,
Qu'une parcelle d'or, dont brille la paillette;
C'est un rêve imprécis, un mirage lointain.
Du ciel qu'on croit tenir, c'est l'image imparfaite
Sur l'eau qu'avait l'enfant dans le creux de sa main.

REFLECTIONS ON THE WATER

The water held in the child's hand
Reflects the sun and heaven's vastness;
Illusory no doubt, an uncertain treasure,
But where can be found perfect happiness?

The child opens his fingers and unplanned
Sadly, all azure in one drop escapes!
The water held in the child's hand
Reflects the sun and heaven's vastness.

Happiness is never, essentially in the human character.
That sliver of gold, a sparkling particle,
It's a vague dream, a distant specter
Of the sky we think we hold, an imperfect idol;
Reflected in the water once held in a child's hand.

HALLUCINATION

Les hauts arbres du parc, la nuit, sur le ciel sombre
Ressemblent aux décors découpés du «Chat Noir»
Alors qu'on y faisait de l'or avec de l'ombre
Et que Salis était seigneur de ce manoir.

La lune qui paraît brusquement nous fait voir,
Galopant, d'Iéna, les cavaliers sans nombre;
Les hauts arbres du parc, la nuit, sur le ciel sombre
Ressemblent aux décors découpés du «Chat Noir».

Puis la lune s'en va, emportant la pénombre
Et la nuit sur le ciel abat son éteignoir.
L'histoire a sa magie, les faits qu'elle dénombre
Se reflètent parfois dans l'antique miroir
Des grands arbres du parc, la nuit, sur le ciel sombre.
Versailles 1911

HALLUCINATION

The tall trees of the park, in the dark sky, at night,
Resemble the cutout shapes of the "Chat Noir"
While we made gold without sunlight
And Salis was lord of this manor.

The moon appearing suddenly brings the sight
Galloping, from Jena, horsemen without number.
The tall trees of the park, in the dark sky, at night,
Resemble the cutout shapes of the "Chat Noir."

The moon then departs, taking the twilight,
And the night sky becomes obscure.
History has its magic, the facts it recites
Are sometimes reflected in the antique mirror
Of the tall trees of the park, in the dark sky at night.
Versailles 1911

BON-SECOURS A L'AURORE

Bon-Secours, accroupi le long de sa colline,
Semble garder la terre où reposent ses morts.
Peu à peu, la Cité, dans l'ombre se dessine
Et ses clochers pointus percent la brume d'or.

Au-dessus du Palais, au-dessus de l'Usine,
Planant sur les vaisseaux qui dorment dans le port,
Bon-Secours, accroupi le long de sa colline,
Semble garder la terre où reposent ses morts.

Le triste voyageur qui dès l'aube chemine
Dans le brouillard glacé, trouve le réconfort
Auprès du Christ doré que l'aurore illumine.
Il quitte avec regret, plus content de son sort
Bon-Secours, accroupi le long de sa colline.

Rouen 1916

BON-SECOURS AT DAWN

Bon-Secours, perched along its bluff,
Appears to guard the ground where its dead rest.
Little by little, the city from shadows defines itself,
As sharp steeples pierce the golden mist.

Above the Palace, above the Factory,
Hovering over the ships asleep in port.
Bon-Secours, perched along its bluff,
Appears to guard the ground where its dead rest.

The unhappy traveler at daybreak walks on
In the freezing fog and finds company
Beside the golden Christ illuminated at dawn.
He leaves with regret but happier with his destiny—
Bon-Secours perched along its bluff.

Rouen 1916

LES NUAGES

Des nuages légers, la caravane agile
Dans les déserts du ciel passe éternellement.
Elle avance sans bruit sur sa route fragile,
Vers un but inconnu elle va lentement.

Parfois pour obéir aux vents fous et futiles
On la voit sans raison sur ses pas revenant.
Des nuages légers, la caravane agile
Dans les déserts du ciel passe éternellement.

L'orgueil nous fait subir des affronts inutiles,
Il faut pour s'élever s'abaisser trop souvent;
Son joug met sur nos fronts sa marque indélébile
Puis nous disparaissons comme au souffle du vent,
Des nuages légers, la caravane agile.

THE CLOUDS

Wispy clouds, in a lively procession
Through a desert sky, pass eternally.
Advancing softly on their fragile progression
Toward an unknown end, they move quietly.

Obeying winds fierce and futile, on occasion,
We see them returning without apology.
Wispy clouds, in a lively procession
Through a desert sky, pass eternally.

Through pride we suffer pointless insult
To elevate ourselves we must often bend.
Its yoke leaves an indelible result
Then we disappear like a gust of wind,
Wispy clouds, in a lively procession.

SAINT-VALERY

Saint-Valery, tu as le charme des vieux bourgs
Qui dorment sur le bord de la mer immortelle.
Tes falaises, au loin, tendent avec amour
Leurs bras, pour enlacer ton amante infidèle.

Du haut de ton clocher semblent tomber toujours
Les longs gémissements d'une plainte éternelle.
Saint-Valery, tu as le charme des vieux bourgs
Qui dorment sur le bord de la mer immortelle.

Quand la nuit sur la terre étend son noir velours
Et que la mer se plaint de n'être plus si belle,
Le phare infatigable, à chacun de ses tours,
Vient sur les toits bleutés mettre son étincelle.
Saint-Valery, tu as le charme des vieux bourgs!

SAINT-VALERY

Saint-Valery, you have the charm of old villages
Who sleep along the seacoast immortal.
Your cliffs reach out in the distance with fondness,
Their arms embrace your lover unfaithful.

The height of your steeple forever messages
The plaintive cries of lament eternal.
Saint-Valery, you have the charm of old villages
Who sleep along the seacoast immortal.

When over the land night spreads its black velvet
And the sea complains, no longer so alluring,
The tireless lighthouse beams ecliptic
And leaves sparks on the blue roofing.
Saint-Valery you have the charm of old villages!

LA GLACE

Dans son cadre doré se tient l'austère glace
Montrant sans flatterie aux hommes ce qu'ils sont.
On ne peut la tromper tant elle est perspicace,
L'infini se reflète en son regard profond.

Chacun vient y briller, s'estompe et puis s'efface,
Elle ne garde rien, c'est un vase sans fond.
Dans son cadre doré se tient l'austère glace
Montrant sans flatterie aux hommes ce qu'ils sont.

    Sur la terre aussi l'homme passe
    Sans laisser durable sillon!
    Le pâle reflet de sa face
    Eclaire un instant d'un rayon
Le monde indifférent, comme l'austère glace.

THE MIRROR

In its golden frame the austere mirror
Shows without flattery men as they are.
It cannot be fooled given its character,
Infinity reflected in its profound stare.

Everyone comes and shines, fades and disappears,
It keeps nothing, it is a bottomless jar.
In its golden frame sits the austere mirror
Showing without flattery men as they are.

    On earth also, man's progression
    Does not leave a lasting impression!
    His face's pale reflection
    Provides only a momentary ray of illumination,
The indifferent world, that austere mirror.

PAYSAGE D'AUTOMNE

Quand l'automne a voilé le ciel de ses brouillards
Comme on tend chez les morts de sombres draperies,
Le soleil impuissant couvre d'un jour blafard
La triste immensité de plaines défleuries.

Les oiseaux migrateurs annoncent leur départ
Du haut des peupliers qui bordent les prairies
Quand l'automne a voilé le ciel de ses brouillards
Comme on tend chez les morts de sombres draperies.

La terre avant les froids, s'habille de brocard
Tout constellé des ors de ses feuilles jaunies,
Joyaux qu'ont assemblé le vent et le hasard;
Elle aime à se couvrir de teintes de féeries
Quand l'automne a voilé le ciel de ses brouillards.

Bourbonne

AUTUMN LANDSCAPE

When autumn has obscured the sky with cloud
As we cover the dead with somber drapery,
An impotent sun creates a pale sky to shroud
The immense sadness of the flowerless prairie.

The migrating birds announce their departure loudly
From atop the poplars that border the prairie,
When autumn has obscured the sky with cloud
As we cover the dead with somber drapery.

The ground, before the frost, is quilted,
Constellated with the gold of yellowing leaves.
Jewels by wind and chance have been united,
It likes to cover itself with enchanted hues
When autumn has obscured the sky with cloud.

Bourbonne

LES EAUX MORTES

L'eau des marais, le soir, s'endort dans la tristesse,
Eau morte où le soleil met des taches de sang;
Immobile miroir, ignorant l'allégresse
Du ciel bleu, qui scintille aux remous des courants.

La brise, apitoyée, apporte une caresse
A la pauvre recluse, et la berce en chantant.
L'eau des marais, le soir, s'endort dans la tristesse,
Eau morte où le soleil met des taches de sang.

L'âme sans idéal, croupit dans la détresse
Et la sombre torpeur des eaux sans mouvement,
Le reflet de là-Haut, qui vers elle s'abaisse
S'éteint sans réveiller son assoupissement....
L'eau des marais, le soir, s'endort dans la tristesse.
Pour Renée P. Bruges

THE DEAD WATERS

The marshland waters, at night, fall asleep in sadness,
Dead water where the sun leaves a bloody trace.
Calm mirror without awareness
Of the blue sky sparkling on the current's face.

The pitying breeze brings a caress
To the poor recluse and sings to her with grace.
The marshland waters, at night, fall asleep in sadness,
Dead water where the sun leaves a bloody trace.

A soul without purpose stagnates in distress
And the somber torpor of the motionless waters,
The reflection of Up there, which lowers toward it
Extinguishes itself without awakening it from its languor...
The marshland waters, at night, fall asleep in sadness.
For Renée P. Bruges

LES VIEUX MURS

Les vieux murs sont couverts de somptueux manteaux
Faits de gueules-de-loup et de pariétaires;
Mais la sombre Arachné prophétesse des maux,
Tend sur ces moribonds de fragiles suaires.

Sur leurs fronts dénudés qu'escaladent les lierres
Les tours montrent encor l'orgueil des féodaux.
Les vieux murs sont couverts de somptueux manteaux
Faits de gueules-de-loup et de pariétaires.

La nature équitable et prêtresse du Beau
Emaille les jardins et les cimetières;
Les fleurs que nous cueillons dans les blés du coteau
Fleurissent aussi bien au bord des ossuaires.
Les vieux murs sont couverts de somptueux manteaux.

THE OLD WALLS

The old walls are covered with a sumptuous canopy
Made of pellitory and snapdragon;
But the dark Arachne, prophetess of calamity,
Spins fragile shrouds over these moribund.

On the bare façades climb the ivy
The towers still show their haughty feudal dignity.
The old walls are covered with a sumptuous canopy
Made of snapdragon and pellitory.

Nature, equitable priestess of Beauty
Adorns both gardens and cemetery;
The flowers we collect on the hills of barley
Flourish just as well around the ossuary.
The old walls are covered with a sumptuous canopy.

LA VIGNE VIERGE

La vigne vierge au bord des balustres se penche
Comme une femme rousse aux longs cheveux ardents,
Des parures de jais rehaussent chaque branche
Qui doucement frissonne aux caresses du vent.

Ses bras, toujours tendus sur la muraille blanche
A l'huis entrebâillé donne l'air accueillant
La vigne vierge au bord des balustres se penche,
Comme une femme rousse aux longs cheveux ardents.

Ses feuilles, un matin, tombent, rouge avalanche,
Sur les degrés, sans bruit, vers le jardin, roulant.
Aux blessures du froid, c'est son sang qui s'épanche,
Alors, les doigts crispés sur le mur, tristement,
La vigne vierge au bord des balustres se penche.

THE INNOCENT VINE

The innocent vine draped along the baluster
Like a woman with long red flaming tresses.
Ornaments of black enhance each member
Who gently shivers in the wind's caresses.

Its arms stretched along the white enclosure
Gives the half-open door a welcoming address.
The innocent vine draped along the baluster
Like a woman with long red flaming tresses.

Its leaves, one morning, fall, a red avalanche
Rolling towards the garden, slowly, silently
Injured by the cold, its blood advances,
Its contorted fingers cling to the wall, sadly,
The innocent vine draped along the baluster.

LES VITRAUX DE SAINT-GODARD ÉCLAIRÉS LA NUIT

J'aime les tons très doux des vitraux assombris
Qui brillent dans la nuit aux flancs des Cathédrales,
Alors qu'un lourd bourdon, en son sommeil surpris,
Sous les coups du sonneur, emplit l'air de ses râles.

Le temps a patiné les ors et les opales,
La pourpre a des éclats par les ans assouplis;
J'aime les tons très doux des vitraux assombris
Qui brillent dans la nuit aux flancs des Cathédrales.

Le Christ sur les autels, entouré de lambris
Lève trop loin de nous sa face triomphale,
Mais toi, Christ aux vitraux, tu te veux amoindri
Pour t'approcher de l'homme à la tare ancestrale
J'aime les tons très doux des vitraux assombris…
Rouen 1913

THE STAINED GLASS WINDOWS OF SAINT-GODARD SHINING AT NIGHT

I love the soft shades of the windows darkened
That glow from the sides of the cathedral at night.
While a heavy bell, startled and frightened
By the bell ringer's blows, fills the air with its gripe.

The golds and opals, time has blackened,
The purple brightness suffers from aged plight.
I love the soft shades of the windows darkened
That glow from the sides of the cathedral at night.

The Christ on the alter, surrounded by wainscot,
Reveals to us at too great a distance his success.
But you, Christ in the windows, you lower your spot
To be closer to man and his age-old weakness.
I love the soft shades of the windows darkened…
Rouen 1913

NOCTURNE

La lune au teint blafard, au rire inquiétant,
Dans l'azur assombri, lentement se promène,
Se montre, disparaît et dessine en passant
Sur les prés endormis d'étranges phénomènes.

De ses rocs désolés, la mort et le néant
Trament leurs noirs complots contre la race humaine.
La lune au teint blafard, au rire inquiétant,
Dans l'azur assombri, lentement se promène.

Aussi malgré l'éclat discret de son croissant,
Bien que sa clarté soit enjôleuse et sereine,
L'âme du moribond et l'âme de l'enfant
Tressaillent, quand la nuit, complice, nous ramène
La lune au teint blafard, au rire inquiétant.

NOCTURNE

The pale moon with its laughter disquieting
In the clouded heavens, slowly wanders.
Shows itself, disappears, and creates in passing
On the sleeping meadows, strange wonders.

From its desolate rocks, death and nothing
Against humanity devise their dark maneuvers.
The pale moon with its laughter disquieting
In the clouded heavens, slowly wanders.

Despite the slender brightness of its crescent,
And though its clarity is calming and alluring,
The soul of the dying and the soul of the innocent
Shiver when the night, its accomplice, brings forth
The pale moon with its laughter disquieting.

INSTANTANÉS PRIS L'HIVER

Sous la neige, dormant frileuse,
Alors que souffle un âpre vent,
La terre, mère douloureuse,
Prépare ses enfantements.

Le soleil met sa touche rose
Sur le bleu vert du ruisseau
Et doucement, sur l'eau, se pose
La mouette auprès des roseaux.

Ferme ton manteau, voyageur
On entend venir la bourrasque
Qui voudrait t'arracher le cœur
Avec ses griffes de Tarasque.

Sous la pâle face lunaire
Voici la tribu des halbrans
Coupant d'un vol triangulaire
Les brumes rouges du couchant.

C'est de diamant que le givre
Orne l'aiguille des sapins,
C'est avec le ton chaud du cuivre
Que le soleil levant les peint.

Portés par la bise du nord,
Les corbeaux flairant une aubaine,
S'abattent sur le perdreau mort,
Point noir tachant la blanche plaine.

Le flocon de neige voltige,
Blême papillon de l'hiver,
Qui s'en va mourir sur la tige
D'un pin, dans le vallon désert.

En rafale tombe la pluie
Dans les vieux nids abandonnés;
Le ciel est barbouillé de suie,
Rentrons chez nous pour tisonner.
                    Janvier 1917

SNAPSHOTS TAKEN IN WINTER

Under the snow, in a dormant shiver
With a bitter wind blowing,
The earth, sorrowful mother,
Prepares a birthing.

The sun gives a rosy caress
To the creek verdigris.
And softly on the water, rests
The seagull near the reeds.

Traveler, close your coat. Hark!
We hear coming the tempest
That wants to rip out your heart
With the claws of Tarasque.

Under the pale face of the moon,
A flock of wild ducks
Cuts through in triangular flight
The red fog of the twilight.

With diamonds the frost honors
And decorates the needles of the fir tree,
With the warm tones of copper
The rising sun paints the filigree.

Carried by the kiss of the north, unpleasant,
The crows scenting gain,
Descend upon the dead pheasant
A dark spot staining the white plain.

Fluttering about, the snowflakes,
Winter's pale butterflies,
Die on the spikes
Of the pine in the deserted valleys.

In gusts falls the rain
Into the old empty nests;
The sky is darkened and stained,
Let us go home to seek comfort and rest.
January 1917

II

IMPRESSIONS BOURGEOISES
BOURGEOIS IMPRESSIONS

L'IMPASSE DESEVEAUX

Cette impasse me plaît, tortueuse et vieillotte
Elle s'enfuit, discrète, entre ses murs lépreux.
Tout y est de travers, l'imprévu est sa note,
Et ses jours de souffrance ont un regard peureux.

Au coin des huis moussus tremblote
Dans l'ombre, un liquide douteux;
Cette impasse me plaît, tortueuse et vieillotte
Elle s'enfuit, discrète, entre ses murs lépreux.

C'est là que tiennent leur parlote
Les gueux, les chiens, les amoureux.
Sur sa porte, un rentier, coiffé de sa calotte,
Montre qu'il est facile à l'homme d'être heureux
Cette impasse me plait, tortueuse et vieillotte.
Rouen

L'IMPASSE DESEVEAUX

This alley pleases me, winding and quaint,
She flees discreetly between its leprous walls.
Everything is crooked, the unexpected awaits,
And its days of suffering have a fearful call.

At the corner of the mossy door oscillates,
In the shadows, a moisture mysterious;
This alley pleases me, winding and quaint,
She flees discreetly between its leprous walls.

It is there they hold their banter,
The beggars, the dogs, and the lovers.
Cap on, at his door, a pensioner
Shows how easy it is for a man to be content.
This alley pleases me, winding and quaint.
Rouen

LE FUMIER

Sur le tas fumier poussent de tendres fleurs,
Ainsi l'a décrété la troublante nature
Qui parfois fait sortir le calme du malheur
Et veut que la vertu engendre l'imposture.

Le coq, grattant le sol de son ergot rageur
Sous le gazon fleuri trouve la pourriture,
Sur le tas fumier poussent de tendres fleurs,
Ainsi l'a décrété la troublante nature.

N'imitons pas le coq, maladroit fureteur,
Pour ne pas affronter les pires aventures,
Et quand s'étend sur nous le voile de bonheur
Evitons de chercher quelle en est la doublure….
Sur le tas de fumier poussent de tendres fleurs.

THE COMPOST

From the pile of compost grows tender greenery
There, illustrates nature's mystery,
Which allows serenity to emerge from calamity,
And wants virtue to beget treachery.

The rooster, scratching the soil furiously
Exposes, under the flowering turf, putridity.
From the pile of compost grows tender greenery
There, illustrates nature's mystery.

Be not like the rooster, clumsy troublemaker,
So as not to encounter misfortune,
And when upon us descends the veil of pleasure
Avoid looking for the inopportune….
From the pile of compost grows tender greenery.

LES JUGES (croquis d'audience)

Sur leurs larges fauteuils, les trois juges assis
Ont l'abord dédaigneux de seigneurs d'importance;
Les voleurs, les escrocs, les amoureux transis,
La dame trop soumise, occupent l'audience.

Leur œil clos, par moments, sort de sa somnolence
Pour jeter dans la salle un regard indécis.
Sur leurs larges fauteuils, les trois juges assis
Ont l'abord dédaigneux de seigneurs d'importance.

Qu'on juge un sacristain ou bien un circoncis,
Que le fait soit douteux ou de jurisprudence,
Qu'un homme ait maraudé, qu'un enfant soit occis,
Digérant doucement, ils dorment en cadence
Sur leurs larges fauteuils, les trois juges assis.

THE JUDGES (a courtroom sketch)

In their large armchairs, the three judges consider,
With the scornful look of important nobility,
The thieves, the swindlers, the nervous lovers,
The downtrodden woman—all attract scrutiny.

Eyes half-closed, they occasionally stir,
Fitfully observing the hall indecisively.
In their large armchairs, the three judges consider,
With the scornful look of important nobility.

Whether judging a cleric or a sinner,
Whether the facts are in doubt or discovered,
Whether a man vandalized or injured a minor,
Digesting tranquilly, they sleep together,
In their large armchairs, the three judges consider.

LE CHEMIN CREUX

Qu'il est joli, le chemin creux,
Semé de fleurs, bordé d'orties,
Qui s'en va, mince et tortueux
Par les guérets et les prairies!

Que m'importe qu'il soit boueux
Les jours où le vient voir la pluie;
Il est joli, le chemin creux,
Semé de fleurs, bordé d'orties.

Là-haut, n'a-t-on pas le ciel bleu?
Et puis, quand l'ornière est franchie,
Le mauvais pas n'est plus qu'un jeu.
C'est là l'image de la vie…
Suivons gaîment son chemin creux.
Boisguillaume

THE SUNKEN TRAIL

The sunken trail is so alluring,
Bordered in nettles, sown with flowers.
Who goes on its way, slender and winding
By the fields, tillage and pastures!

Who cares if they are muddying
On the days of rain showers?
The sunken trail is so alluring,
Bordered in nettles, sown with flowers.

Above, do we not have a blue sky endearing?
And when a rut is confronted,
The bad step is part of the undertaking.
Here is life represented…
Let's gaily follow its sunken trail so alluring.
Boisguillaume

LES VIELLES MAISONS

Comme des aïeules frileuses,
A l'âtre se chauffant les doigts,
Elles se courbent, douloureuses,
Les branlantes maisons de bois.

Que de drames, que de mystères
Elles ont vu se dérouler!
Que de bonheurs! Que de misères!
Combien de larmes ont coulé!

La vieillesse est peu quinteuse,
Elle méprise l'avenir,
Et dans son passé vit heureuse.
Pour se conter leurs souvenirs

Par-dessus l'impasse boueuse,
Mêlant l'imprévu de leurs toits,
Elles se courbent douloureuses,
Les branlantes maisons de bois!

Mais dans leur âme rajeunie
Par les images du passé
Renaît la tendresse alanguie
Des anciens jours. Pour s'embrasser
Quand de sa lourde voix grondeuse
Le couvre-feu sonne au beffroi,
Elles se courbent douloureuses,
Les branlantes maisons de bois.

ENVOI
Architecte, grand destructeur,
Laisse vivre ces pauvres vieilles.
Tu n'as pas toujours le bonheur
De nous construire des merveilles!
Rouen 1913

OLD HOUSES

Like shivering grandmothers
Warming themselves by the fire,
They bend, aching,
These tired, rickety houses of wood.

What dramas, what mysteries
They witnessed unfold!
What happiness! What miseries!
How many tears have flowed!

Old age can be a bit cranky
She distrusts destiny,
And in her past, lives contentedly
Recounting her memories.

Over the dead-end alley muddy and forsaken
The massed angles of their roofs in jumbled method,
They bend, aching,
These tired, rickety houses of wood.

But in their spirit, revived
By the images of the past,
The languid tenderness is recovered
Of the old days. To embrace,
As the belfry, its heavy voice grumbling,
Announces the quieting neighborhood,
They bend, aching,
These tired, rickety houses of wood.

ENVOI

Architect, grand destroyer,
Let live these elders.
You don't always have the pleasure
Of building us such wonders!

Rouen 1913

A LA CRÈME!
FROMAGE A LA CRÈME!...

Voile de mousseline et petit cœur tout blanc,
Vers la ville s'en va le fromage à la crème
Dans le panier du vieux qui s'éloigne en chantant
Sa plaintive chanson, quand rosit l'aube blême.

Avec un petit pain, il compose souvent
Un somptueux festin au pays de Bohême,
Voile de mousseline et petit cœur tout blanc,
Vers la ville s'en va le fromage à la crème.

Il tremble au moindre heurt, il est tendre, innocent,
Fragile, sans défense, et c'est pourquoi je l'aime.
Dans son berceau d'osier on dirait un enfant
Dormant sur des coussins, en robe de baptême…
Voile de mousseline et petit cœur tout blanc!
Senlis

FRESH!
FRESH CHEESE!...

Veil of muslin and a small white heart
The fresh cheese goes to the city
In the basket of the elder who sings traveling to market
His plaintive song, as the pale dawn grows in intensity.

With a little bread, he often starts
A sumptuous feast in the idyllic country.
Veil of muslin and a small, white heart,
The fresh cheese goes to the city.

With the slightest bump, he trembles, he is innocent,
Fragile, without defense, and that is why I love him.
In his wicker basket, he is like an infant
Sleeping on cushions with baptismal trim…
Veil of muslin and a small, white heart!
Senlis

LA VIGNE DES COTEAUX DE BOURBONNE
(chant de terroir)

La vigne s'élance en bataille
A l'escalade du coteau.
Elle a des baudriers de paille
Et pour fusil, le fin paisseau.

La grive quittant sa ripaille
A plein gosier sonne l'assaut.
La vigne s'élance en bataille
A l'escalade du coteau.

Septembre alourdit la grenaille
Des raisins, aux flancs du Pineau.
Le Gamay suit, fruste et canaille
Le sang vermeil à fleur de peau.
La vigne s'élance en bataille!...

THE VINE OF THE HILLS OF BOURBONNE
(song of the soil)

The vine throws itself into the fray
And aggressively climbs the ridge.
She has bandoliers of hay
And for a rifle, slender treillage.

Leaving its feast, the jay
Announces the assault with high pitch.
The vine throws itself into the fray
And aggressively climbs the ridge.

September augments the weight
Of the grapes, Pineau noticeably.
Gamay follows suit, rough and gay
The red blood ready to flow copiously.
The vine throws itself into the fray!...

LE VIEUX POT A ONGUENT

Le nez de Cyrano, le ventre d'un notaire
Ont servi de modèle au vieux pot à onguent,
Qui dort sur le dressoir en un lit de poussière
Entre la bassinoire et le plat de Rouen.

Sur le front craquelé de valétudinaire
L'abandon a mis plus de rides que les ans.
Le nez de Cyrano, le ventre d'un notaire
Ont servi de modèle au vieux pot à onguent.

Jadis, au temps béni des Purgons de Molière
Des cérats onctueux, des tendres liniments,
Il trônait orgueilleux chez un apothicaire
Et, respecté de tous, il portait noblement
Le nez de Cyrano, le ventre d'un notaire.

THE OLD OINTMENT POT

The belly of a notary, the nose of Cyrano
The old ointment pot resembles.
In a bed of dust, it sleeps on the bureau
Between the basin and plate from Rouen, it crumbles.

On its ailing face, cracks of sorrow,
Abandonment has added more than age, wrinkles.
The belly of a notary, the nose of Cyrano
The old ointment pot resembles.

Long ago in the blessed times of the Purgons of Moliere
Filled with the unctuous cerates, delicate remedies,
He ruled proudly at the apothecary,
And respected by all, he carried nobly
The nose of Cyrano, the belly of a notary.

LA LAITIÈRE

Dans la blancheur du lait, l'œil noir de la laitière,
Charbon dans de la neige est d'un contraste heureux,
Qu'il vienne de Grenade ou de la Cannebière,
C'est du midi que vient ce velours ténébreux.

Au temps de d'Artagnan, au temps des Grieux,
En l'honneur d'un tel œil on tirait la rapière!
Dans la blancheur du lait, l'œil noir de la laitière,
Charbon dans de la neige est d'un contraste heureux.

De l'époque héroïque on n'a plus la manière,
Finis les coups d'estoc, finis les songe-creux!
Manon participe aux retraites ouvrières,
Et seuls, quelques rêveurs chantent en vers boiteux
Dans la blancheur du lait, l'œil noir de la laitière!
Ville-d'Avray

THE MILKMAID

Against the whiteness of the milk, the dark eyes of the milkmaid,
Coal in the snow is a pleasing comparison.
Whether from Grenada or Cannebiere conveyed
From the south, comes this velvet black creation.

In the times of D'Artagnan and of des Gieux; easily swayed
For the honor of such an eye, swords and confrontation!
Against the whiteness of the milk, the dark eyes of the milkmaid,
Coal in the snow is a pleasing comparison.

No longer do we live in such a heroic age.
Gone the cut and thrust, gone the romantics!
Manon now receives the workers' wages,
And few, the dreamers, sing with shaky lyrics
Of the whiteness of the milk, the dark eyes of the milkmaid!
Ville-d'Avray

L'HORLOGE DU LOUVRE

De son tic-tac discret, l'horloge dans la nuit
Au nom du bon vieux temps compte chaque seconde,
Et mesure les pas de l'heure qui s'enfuit
Menant vers l'inconnu le char pesant du monde.

Au cœur désabusé que torture l'ennui
Par son charme berceur la peine est moins profonde.
De son tic-tac discret, l'horloge dans la nuit
Au nom du bon vieux temps compte chaque seconde.

Mais pour le criminel que le sommeil a fui
Son balancier vengeur semble mener la ronde
Des remords, dont la meute en hurlant le poursuit.
Enfin! seule elle a vu décamper la Joconde,
A petits pas discrets, l'horloge dans la nuit!

THE CLOCK OF THE LOUVRE

With its discreet tick-tock, the clock at night
In the interest of keeping time counts each second sown,
And measures the footsteps of time's flight
Moving the weight of the world toward the unknown.

A disillusioned tortured heart in its plight
Will find sorrow lessened by the charming tone,
With its discreet tick-tock, the clock at night
In the interest of keeping time counts each second sown.

But for the criminal who cannot sleep
The avenging pendulum undertakes the fight
Reminding him of the regrets he keeps.
Ah! It alone witnessed the Mona Lisa take flight
By soft little footsteps, the clock at night!

Historical footnote: The Mona Lisa was stolen from the Louvre in 1911.

LE DIVAN LOUIS-PHILIPPE

Le divan Louis-Philippe avait l'air étonné
Lorsque sur son velours, hier, tu t'es assise,
Frôlant son acajou rigide et suranné,
Des contours vaporeux de ta robe imprécise.

Jadis, sur ses ressorts, venaient, pour badiner,
Le pantalon à pont et la basquine bise.
Le divan Louis-Philippe avait l'air étonné
Lorsque sur son velours, hier, tu t'es assise.

L'homme garde l'amour du siècle où il est né;
Des falbalas d'antan son âme reste éprise;
Et je comprends pourquoi, pauvre déraciné,
Voyant ta jupe étroite et ta robe chemise,
Le divan Louis-Philippe avait l'air étonné…

Pour Mme R. G. Rouen

THE LOUIS-PHILIPPE DIVAN

The Louis-Philippe divan looked astonished
When, yesterday, you sat on its velvet,
Brushing against mahogany rigid and outdated,
With your dress vaporous and ill-defined.

On its springs, bantering now vanished,
Pleated pants and petticoats met.
The Louis-Philippe divan looked astonished
When yesterday, you sat on its velvet.

Man loves the age he is born to possess;
To frills of yore, his spirit will attest.
So I understand why, this unfortunate dispossessed,
Seeing your narrow skirt and nightgown dress,
The Louis-Philippe divan appeared astonished….

For Mrs. R.G. Rouen

LE BALAYEUR

D'un geste indifférent et las, le balayeur
Promène son balai, grave comme un augure.
Sans souci des saisons, éternel moissonneur
Fauchant sur les pavés sa récolte d'ordures.

Pour calmer du soleil la déprimante ardeur,
De la source cachée il fait jaillir l'eau pure.
D'un geste indifférent et las, le balayeur
Promène son balai, grave comme un augure.

Des tendres sentiments, sinistre fossoyeur
Il entasse impassible, au fond de sa voiture,
La lettre où l'on a mis le meilleur de son cœur
Avec les reliefs d'odieuses fritures…
D'un geste indifférent et las, le balayeur.

THE SWEEPER

His moves indifferent and languid, the sweeper
Walks with his broom, serious as an augur.
Indifferent to the season, this eternal reaper
Sweeps the stones, and harvests the litter.

To provide relief from the sun's oppressing fever
From a hidden source he releases pure water.
His moves indifferent and languid, the sweeper
Walks with his broom, serious as an augur.

The tender sentiments, this sinister undertaker
Collects impassively in his carrier,
The heartfelt letters, the best of our character,
Mixed together with odious litter…
His moves indifferent and languid, the sweeper.

III

LES JARDINS
THE GARDENS

LES JARDINS

D'aucuns jugent les gens par les plis de la main
Par le marc de café, par la carte étalée
D'un tarot fatidique. A de subtils devins
Par un seul mot écrit, notre âme est dévoilée.

Pourquoi n'a-t-on jamais cherché dans les jardins
Ce que peut refléter la courbe d'une allée?
On juge bien les gens par les plis de la main,
Par le marc de café, par la carte étalée!

Ce jardin trop soigné montre un esprit mesquin;
Un fantasque a conçu l'allure échevelée
De ce hardi massif. Par ces signes certains
Notre mentalité se trouve révélée
Bien mieux que par les plis tracés dans notre main.

THE GARDENS

By the lines on their hands, some judge others,
By coffee grounds, by cards revealed
By fateful tarot. To subtle soothsayers,
By a single written word, our soul is unveiled.

Can we not look at gardens to discover
What can be properly reflected?
By the lines on their hands, some judge others,
By coffee grounds, by cards revealed!

A manicured garden shows the reactionary;
The delusional creates an arrangement disheveled.
By these peculiarities and certainties
Our mindset is revealed more effectively
Than by tracing the lines on our hands unwisely.

LE VIEUX JARDIN

Rien ne vaut la douceur triste du vieux jardin
Qui végète, assoupi dans sa mélancolie
Et qui semblè écouter quelque clocher lointain
Contant les souvenirs d'une époque abolie.

Auprès du fier soleil, du phlox dur et hautain
Tremble la clématite en sa grâce amollie.
Rien ne vaut la douceur triste du vieux jardin
Qui végète, assoupi dans sa mélancolie.

Entre les buis taillés, c'est là, frêle et jolie
Que la belle-de-nuit regarde avec dédain
La nigelle aux yeux bleus; que la tendre ancolie
Dans ses urnes reçoit les larmes du matin…
Rien ne vaut la douceur triste du vieux jardin!
Pour Ph. Bourbonne-les Bains, Juin 1913

THE OLD GARDEN

Nothing compares to the sad sweetness of the old garden
Which vegetates, dozing in its melancholy,
To a distant bell it seems to hearken
Reawakening memories of a bygone history.

Facing the proud sun, next to phlox, haughty and hardened
Trembles the clematis, with softened beauty.
Nothing compares to the sad sweetness of the old garden
Which vegetates, dozing in its melancholy.

Between the carved boxwood, there, fragile and lovely
The marvel of Peru looks scorning
At the blue-eyed nigella; that the columbine dainty
In its urns receives the tears of the morning…
Nothing compares to the sad sweetness of the old garden!
For Ph. Bourbonne-les-Bains, June 1913

LE JARDIN POTAGER

*Sur sa couche, effondré, s'arrondit le melon
Qui règne au potager avec dame citrouille;
Le couple est imposant, bien qu'il soit sans façon,
On dirait deux soleils couchants vêtus de rouille.*

*En voyant approcher la tribu des oignons,
L'asperge au long cou blanc sent son œil qui mouille.
Sur sa couche, effondré, s'arrondit le melon
Qui règne au potager avec dame citrouille.*

*Sur les choux, l'arrosoir verse des cabochons,
Le haricot s'enroule de la quenouille
Des échalas; dans l'eau s'agite le cresson;
L'homme au tablier bleu près des plants s'agenouille.
Sur sa couche, effondré, s'arrondit le melon.*

THE VEGETABLE GARDEN

Collapsed in his bed, fattens the cantaloupe, crushingly,
Who, with the dame pumpkin, rules the garden.
An imposing couple, despite being homely,
They appear to be two sunsets draped in titian.

Observing the tribe of onions approaching,
The long white-necked asparagus feels her eyes moisten.
Collapsed in his bed, fattens the cantaloupe, crushingly,
Who, with the dame pumpkin, rules the garden.

On the cabbage, the watering can pours sparkle and zest,
The green beans curl around their station.
In the trench, stirs the watercress;
The man with the blue apron kneels near the vegetation.
Collapsed in his bed, fattens the cantaloupe, crushingly.

LE JARDIN ABANDONNÉ

Tristes sont les allées où l'on ne passe plus,
Qui dorment près de la demeure abandonnée,
Sur leurs bords sont plantés de vieux tilleuls moussus
Comme des sphinx assis auprès d'un hypogée.

Les lichens ont rongé les étais vermoulus
De la porte inutile aux ferrures rouillées.
Tristes sont les allées où l'on ne passe plus,
Qui dorment près de la demeure abandonnée!

Sous le souffle du vent d'un essor éperdu,
Si l'on voit s'envoler les feuilles apeurées,
C'est qu'elles ont appris des pauvres disparus
Les secrets implacables de la destinée...
Tristes sont les allées où l'on ne passe plus!

Mont-Saint-Aignan 1914

THE ABANDONED GARDEN

Sad are the paths no longer trodden
That sleep near the dwelling abandoned.
On the side are planted mossy linden
Who, sphinx-like, sit near the hypogeum.

Lichens have gnawed the frame, moldy and sodden,
Of the useless door with nails rusty and stranded.
Sad are the paths no longer trodden
That sleep near the dwelling abandoned.

By the buffeted remains of efforts misbegotten,
We see the windblown flight of frightened leaves.
They have learned from the wretched forgotten
The merciless secrets of destiny...
Sad are the paths no longer trodden!

Mont-Saint-Aignan 1914

LE JARDIN PUBLIC

Pomponné, bichonné comme une femmelette,
Que le jardin public est triste et ennuyeux!
Offrant à tout venant sa grâce de coquette
Il est le paradis rêvé du loqueteux.

Ses bancs de bois verdâtre écoutent la causette
De l'enfant, du soldat, du retraité goutteux.
Pomponné, bichonné comme une femmelette,
Que le jardin public est triste et ennuyeux!

A songer à ce parc, on a l'âme inquiète:
Quel contraste effrayant entre ces miséreux
Qui ne vivent jamais que des jours de disette
Et leur jardin trop riche, insolent, luxueux,
Pomponné, bichonné comme une femmelette.

THE PUBLIC GARDEN

Pampered and primped like a sissy,
How sad and annoying is the public garden!
Offering to all its flirty beauty,
It is a dream come true for the broken.

The greenish benches listen to chatter spoken foolishly,
Of the soldier, the gouty retirees, and the children.
Pampered and primped like a sissy,
How sad and annoying is the public garden!

To think of this park upsets one's disposition:
What a frightening contrast between these, the hopeless,
Who live lives of such destitution
And their garden too elegant, insolent, luxurious,
Pampered and primped like a sissy.

LE JARDIN DU CURÉ

*Un jardin pacifique orne le presbytère
Qu'étreint un chèvrefeuille aux bras capricieux;
Entr'ouvert, sur un banc, bâille le bréviaire
Près duquel, au soleil, s'étire un chat frileux.*

*La main dans la ceinture, auprès de son vicaire,
Le curé voit mûrir l'abricot savoureux;
Un jardin pacifique orne le presbytère
Qu'étreint un chèvrefeuille aux bras capricieux.*

*Le fossoyeur, lassé, quitte le cimetière
Pour planter des radis. Sous un platane ombreux
La vierge au doux sourire étend ses mains de mère
Et verse l'espérance au cœur des malheureux…
Un jardin pacifique orne le presbytère.*

THE PRIEST'S GARDEN

A peaceful garden adorns the presbytery
Embraced by a wide-armed honeysuckle tree;
Half-opened, on a bench, yawns the breviary
Near which, in the sun, stretches a cat lazily.

With hand on his rope belt, alongside his vicar,
The priest watches the apricots ripen with scrutiny.
A peaceful garden adorns the presbytery
Embraced by a wide-armed honeysuckle tree.

The gravedigger wearily leaves the cemetery
To plant his radishes. Under a shady sycamore,
The Virgin, with a soft smile, extends her hospitality
And pours hope into the heart of the unfortunate poor…
A peaceful garden adorns the presbytery.

LES JARDINS SUSPENDUS

Il est un charme étrange aux jardins suspendus,
Audacieux défi jeté à la matière;
Où l'arbuste se sent perdu
Loin de la terre nourricière.

C'est l'attrait du fruit défendu,
Du chemin sortant de l'ornière.
Il est un charme étrange aux jardins suspendus,
Audacieux défi jeté à la matière.

La fumée enroulant ses anneaux distendus
Monte comme l'encens de l'humble chaumière.
Du coq résonne au loin l'appel inattendu…
L'homme rêve en silence, ivre de lumière.
Il est un charme étrange aux jardins suspendus.

HANGING GARDENS

There is a strange charm to hanging gardens,
A bold challenge issued to standard positions,
Where plants feel lost, suspended,
Far from the Earth's nourishing conditions.

It is the appeal of the fruit forbidden,
The way out of the quotidian.
There is a strange charm to hanging gardens,
A bold challenge issued to standard positions.

The smoke winding in loose rings
From the humble cottage, climbs like incense.
The unexpected echoes of the rooster faraway calling…
The man dreams in silence, in drunken luminescence.
There is a strange charm to hanging gardens.

LES PETITS JARDINS DES ENVIRONS DE PARIS

Il vous fait rire; Il m'attendrit
Ce jardinet miniature
Qu'auprès des portes de Paris
Le bourgeois taille à sa mesure.

N'est-il pas l'ex-voto fleuri
Qu'un cœur simple offre à la nature?
Il vous fait rire; Il m'attendrit
Ce jardinet miniature…

Son plan, de longs jours a mûri
Dans le tréfonds d'une âme obscure,
Il est le port, il est l'abri
Où l'homme inquiet se rassure:
Il vous fait rire, il m'attendrit!

THE LITTLE GARDENS AROUND PARIS

It makes you laugh; it moves me,
These gardens in miniature.
That, near the gates of Paris, similarly,
Do the bourgeois reveal their character.

A flowering votive offering this could be
That a simple heart offers to nature?
It makes you laugh, it moves me,
These gardens in miniature…

This plot took many days to mature
In the darkness of a soul obscure,
A safe harbor to feel secure
Where a worried mind seeks to reassure:
It makes you laugh, it moves me!

LE CIMETIÈRE AUTOUR DE
L'ÉGLISE DERNIER JARDIN

Le calme et le silence habitent ce jardin
Où l'heure, en sanglotant, comme une larme glisse
Des trous noirs du clocher. Après le grand chagrin
Il faut qu'un cœur blessé enfin se ressaisisse;

L'homme supporte mieux le coup d'un deuil certain
Qu'un malheur attendu, perpétuel supplice!
Le calme et le silence habitent ce jardin
Où l'heure, en sanglotant, comme une larme glisse.

Au-dessus du cyprès s'élève le sapin
Symbole de l'espoir, et sous l'ombre propice
Du clocher des aïeux, il est d'ordre divin
Qu'à l'âme des vivants l'esprit des morts s'unisse.
Le calme et le silence habitent ce jardin...
Choiseul

THE CEMETERY OUTSIDE THE CHURCH THE LAST GARDEN

Silence inhabits this garden's calmness
Where time, weeping, like a tear descends
From the dark windows of the bell tower. After sadness,
A wounded heart must finally mend.

Man bears better the sudden blow of distress
Than a slow and sure affliction, torment with no end!
Silence inhabits this garden's calmness
Where time, weeping, like a tear descends.

Above the cypress rises the fir tree,
Symbol of hope, and under the auspicious height
Of the ancestral bell tower, it is divinely ordered to be
That the soul of the living and the spirit of the dead unite.
Silence inhabits this garden's calmness…
Choiseul

LE JARDIN SECRET

Tout homme au fond du cœur a son jardin secret
Où jamais le profane odieux ne pénètre.
Temple charmant. Temple discret
Dont on est soi-même le prêtre.

Sous son triple verrou, mystérieux coffret
Qui ne peut s'entr'ouvrir que sous la main du maitre,
Tout homme au fond du cœur a son jardin secret
Où jamais le profane odieux ne pénètre.

Les fruits de ce jardin sont quelquefois mauvais:
Tristes déchets de vie, ou biens legs d'un ancêtre.
La Parque au front ridé veut que son rouet
Le fils rugueux du chanvre au fil d'or s'enchevêtre..
Tout homme au fond du cœur a son jardin secret.

THE SECRET GARDEN

All men in their hearts have their secret garden
Where never can enter an unholy entity.
Sacred temple, temple guarded
Where we are our own authority.

Under triple locks, this mysterious chest, hardened,
Can only be opened by its owner carefully.
All men in their hearts have their secret garden
Where never can enter an unholy entity.

The fruits of this garden are sometimes regrettable:
Ancestral legacy or the sad debris of one's lifetime.
Parca,* with furrowed brow, tries on her trundle
To weave the rough thread of hemp with golden twine.
All men in their hearts have their secret garden.

**Parca – a goddess in ancient Roman mythology who directed the lives*
and deaths of humans.

LE VASE DE MARBRE

Les nymphes des bosquets, en blanches théories
Dansent pour le plaisir des héros et des dieux;
Et c'est en contemplant ces pâles effigies
Qu'on trouve le secret de l'âme des aïeux
Qui entouraient l'amour, la jeunesse, la vie,
La femme et la beauté de mille soins pieux.
Les nymphes des bosquets, en blanches théories
Dansent pour le plaisir des héros et des dieux.

Les satyres barbus, lorgnent avec envie
Sur les anses, juchés, le cortège joyeux;
Leur face où sont unis le vice et l'ironie
Donne encor plus d'attraits aux corps voluptueux
Souples et alignés en blanche théories.
Versailles 1913

THE MARBLE VASE

The nymphs of the gardens, dressed in ivory
For the pleasure of heroes and gods, dance merrily,
And in contemplating these pale effigies,
The secret soul of the ancients is revealed artfully.
They embrace love, life, vitality,
Women, beauty, and a thousand precious qualities.
The nymphs of the gardens, dressed in ivory
For the pleasure of heroes and gods, dance merrily.

The bearded satyrs leer with envy
On the handles, they watch the joyous harmony;
Their faces display both vice and irony
Accentuating the voluptuous bodies,
Supple and well-formed, dressed in ivory.
Versailles 1913

LES FLEURS DES TALUS

Au grand soleil d'été, certes la plaine est belle;
Elle montre sa force et prouve sa grandeur
Par son frémissement d'indomptable rebelle
Imposant à son maître un éternel labeur.
Sa richesse s'étale en bandes symétriques;
Ses guérets, ses moissons, ses vergers et ses champs,
Composent sur le sol de riches mosaïques
Dont on admire l'ordre et les tons éclatants.
Le bœuf, au pas tranquille, à l'échine fumante
A parcouru le sol, guidé par l'aiguillon
  Et voilà que la terre enfante
  Du blé tout le long des sillons.

  Qui n'admire la symphonie
  Des fleurs qui peuplent les jardins
  Et la docte polychromie
  De nos parterres citadins
  Mais ce ne sont que des captives
  Que l'homme conduit par la main
  On entend leur âme craintive
  Gémissant sous sa loi d'airain.
Plaignons ces pauvres fleurs que le destin fit naître
Recluses de harem, sans personnalité,
Odalisques voulant attirer l'œil du maître
Par leur soumission et leur fidélité.

  Mais voilà qu'un matin d'automne
  Des graines prennent leur essor
  Fuyant la terre monotone
  Où l'on doit vivre sans effort.
  Les plus fortes, les plus heureuses,
  Trouvent le sol libérateur,
  Ce talus des routes poudreuses

Qui est l'Amérique des fleurs.
Elles germent dans les tranchées
Que creusa le pas d'un cheval,
Et dans les rigoles tracées
Le long de chemin vicinal.

Leur gaité, leur entrain effacent leurs tristesses
Le tendre vent du sud, l'âpre bise du nord
Leur donnent des soufflets que suivent des caresses;
Elles servent de lit au chemineau qui dort;
L'égoïste frelon et l'abeille sauvage
Y butinent l'été le pollen savoureux,
Et vont cacher là-bas leur onctueux breuvage
Dans les celliers construits au fond d'un arbre creux.

Sur un tapis de violettes
On voit s'avancer deux géants:
La digitale aux cent clochettes
Et le timide bouillon-blanc.
Dans le coin voisinent la menthe
Le serpolet, le thym des champs,
L'absinthe à l'haleine puissante
Et l'anis odoriférant.

Pleines de dignité, ces fleurs officinales
Avec des sucs choisis composent leurs liqueurs,
Elles ont revêtu des robes monacales,
Moyen, chacun le sait, d'attirer l'acheteur.
Balançant une ombrelle blanche
Au-dessus de son corps fluet,
Le panais sauvage se penche
Et danse un pas de menuet.
Prolifique, le séneçon,
Au vent disperse ses houppettes,
C'est avec la fleur du mouron

La manne des bergeronnettes.
Ce fier-à-bras, un peu godiche,
Armé de dards, c'est le chardon;
Ornant le col d'une potiche
Il finira dans un salon.

La fraise fleurit dans le sable,
Le pavot s'incline, poli,
Devant le couple délectable,
De la mâche et du pissenlit.
L'hiver, dans les jours de disette,
Que deviendraient sans le plantain
Le rouge-gorge et la fauvette?
Ils n'auraient qu'à mourir de faim!
Lorsque la saison des froids cesse,
La fougère, entre les cailloux
Elève sa crosse d'abbesse
Aux ciselures de bijou.
Puis le coucou, la primevère
La marguerite et le bleuet
Gaité de la lande en jachère
Se hasardent sur les guérets.
Mais que vient la ciguë
Auprès de ces honnêtes fleurs?
Arrachons la feuille exiguë
De ce faux persil de malheur!
Tout autour de la colonie,
La ronce aux rameaux annelés
Dresse la frise en dents de scie
De ses fils de fer barbelés.

Il est des gens aussi dont l'âme se mutine
Alors que l'Etat veut les mettre en espalier…,
Qui ont horreur de l'ordre, haïssent la routine,

Le sécateur et le fumier.
Pour ces gens, la vie a sa marge,
Ses à côtés et ses talus,
Que c'est haut si ce n'est pas large
Dans ce domaine des élus!
C'est la Thébaïde accueillante
Aux songes sans fin des rêveurs,
L'asile où la vie est calmante
Loin des plaisirs et des honneurs.
La poésie et la musique,
Le cher livre trop vite lu
Voilà toute la politique
Gouvernant l'homme des talus!

ENVOI

De quelque façon qu'on te nomme,
Ou cardinal, ou prince, ou gueux,
Puisque tu n'es jamais qu'un homme
Il te faudra pour être heureux
Rechercher l'équité, jamais le bénéfice,
Mépriser l'intrigant et le laisser passer,
Redouter la faveur autant que l'injustice,
Te courber sous l'orage et puis te redresser,
Eviter l'optimisme et la mélancolie,
Admirer le soir sombre et le matin vermeil,
Te choisir une place au talus de la vie
Les pieds dans les cailloux, mais la tête au soleil!
Bourbonne, Septembre 1920

THE FLOWERS OF THE EMBANKMENTS

Under the hot summer sun, the plain is certainly beautiful;
It shows its power and proves its grandeur
In the way it undulates like an untamable rebel
Imposing on her master an eternal labor.
Its riches extend in symmetrical bands
And forms on the earth a rich mosaic,
Its harvests, orchards, fields, the toiled land
Admired for its order and the brilliant tone it takes.
The ox with quiet steps and steaming back
Has traveled the ground driven by blows,
    And here, the black fertile earth gives birth
    To wheat all along the furrows.

    Who doesn't admire the symphony
    Of the flowers in gardens growing,
    And the cultivated pattern motley
    Of the urban flower beds overflowing.
    But these are only captives
    That man leads by the hand.
    In plaintive cries we hear of this
    Whimpering under his heavy commands.
Pity these poor flowers born unto this destiny
To be recluses of the harem, without personality,
Odalisques seeking attention and empathy
By their submission and loyalty.

    But come one autumn morning,
    The seeds take flight
    From the dull earth, fleeing
    A life mundane, without plight.
    The happiest, the strongest
    Find liberated terrain,
    In ridges and dusty roads they belong.

An America for flowers they attain.
They germinate in trenches
Carved by a horse's hoofs,
In traced gullies and edges
Along country paths, aloof.

Their joy and high spirits overcome their sadness
The soft southern wind, the bitter kiss from the north
A bond is created from these caresses;
A bed for the vagabond brought forth;
The selfish hornet and savage bee
Forage for the summer pollen,
And hide their oily beverage carefully
In cellars carved from the tree trunks sodden.

On a carpet of violets
Two giants reign:
The foxglove with a hundred bonnets
And the timid white mullein.
In this corner, mint so neighborly
With wild thyme, thyme of the fields,
The absinthe of powerful scent savory
And sweet fragrant anise revealed.

Full of dignity, these officinal flowers
Make their liquors with chosen sugars,
In monastic robes themselves covered
To attract, as everyone knows, buyers.
Balancing a white parasol
Over her body feeble and wet,
The wild parsnip rolls
And dances a minuet.
Prolific, the groundsel
Disperses her puffs in the wind,
And with the flower of the pimpernel

Their manna the wagtails find.
This bully, a bit out of place,
A golden thistle with darts drawn,
Soon will be adorning the rim of the vase,
He will end up in a salon.
The strawberries in the sand huddle,
The poppy politely leans in,
Facing the delectable couple
Of the lettuce and dandelion.
In winter, during the days of scarcity
What would happen without plants?
What becomes of the robin's destiny?
He would die of hunger with no chance!
With the cold season's demise
Between the stones, the ferns
Its abbess staff it rises
With jeweled ornate turns.
Then the cowslip, the primrose
The daisy, and the blueberries
In the resting pastures grow
And in the fields make merry.
Why does hemlock appear
Among these honest flowers?
Remove those small leaves drear
Of this false parsley so dour!
All around the colony,
The blackberry with branches entwined
Adorns the scene sharply
With its barbed wire much maligned.
There are people who are also rebellious
Although the state wants to control and contain…,
Those who dislike order, routine, the trellis,
Pruning shears, the muck, the ball and chain.
For these people, life must have an edge,

Cliffs, precipices, and chasms interwoven.
It must be high and right to the ledge
In this domain of the chosen!
It is a Thebaid inviting
With dreams without end for dreamers,
An asylum, where life is soothing
Far from honors and pleasures.
Music and poetry,
The cherished book too quickly read
There is all the polity
Governing men on the edge!

ENVOI

However you are chosen,
A cardinal, prince, or mendicant,
Since you are never more than a person,
Find your own way to be content.
Research justice, without prejudice,
Scorn the schemer, he is wanton,
Fear favoritism as much as injustice,
Bend in a storm and then straighten,
Avoid excess optimism, sadness and strife,
Admire the quiet evening and morning vermilion,
Choose your place at the edge of life
With feet on the ground, but head in the heavens!
Bourbonne, September 1920

IV

LES PARFUMS
FRAGRANCE

LE NEZ – GRAND-MAITRE DES PARFUMS

Grand-maître des parfums, margrave des odeurs,
Nez! Tu veilles toujours, prudent et perspicace.
Bien campé, tu te tiens à ton poste d'honneur,
Droit, entre les deux yeux, au centre de la face!

Que tu sois court ou long, bonhomme ou batailleur,
Chez l'homme et chez le chien, tu es signe de race:
Grand-maître des parfums, margrave des odeurs,
Nez! Tu veilles toujours, prudent et perspicace.

Par ton pouvoir magique, étrange évocateur,
On sent tout l'océan dans un souffle qui passe…
Tu prends dans tes filets l'âme errante des fleurs
Qui s'arrête un moment, nous charme et puis s'efface.
Grand-maître des parfums, margrave des odeurs!

THE NOSE – GRANDMASTER OF PERFUMES

Grandmaster of perfumes, marquis of scents,
Nose! Always on guard, vigilant and clever.
Well positioned, you hold your post with confidence,
Straight, between the eyes, front and center!

Whether short or long, gentle or truculent,
For man and canine, you identify their character.
Grandmaster of perfumes, marquis of scents,
Nose! Always on guard, vigilant and clever.

Strange evocator, by your magical powers
We smell the entire ocean in a breeze fleeting.
You take in your web the wandering soul of flowers
That pause, beguile and then are vanishing.
Grandmaster of perfumes, marquis of scents!

LE CIERGE QUI S'ÉTEINT

Du cierge mourant, la tremblante fumée
Mêle son âcre odeur aux notes du plain-chant;
Et puis, on n'entend plus, dans l'église fermée,
Que des vieux bois meurtris les longs gémissements.

Les senteurs que répand la mêche consumée
Evoquent dans nos cœurs mille tableaux poignants.
Du cierge mourant, la tremblante fumée
Mêle son âcre odeur aux notes du plain-chant.

Du baptême à la mort, la vie est résumée
Dans ce fade parfum vers les voûtes montant;
Quand on songe aux relais dont la vie est semée,
On trouve au souvenir triste ou gai se mêlant,
Du cierge jauni la tremblante fumée.

THE DYING CANDLE

From the dying candle, the trembling smoke
Mixes its acrid odor with the plainchant singing:
Then, from the empty church no further note,
Except the aged and worn wood groaning.

From the aromas of the spent wick, the scent evokes
In our hearts a thousand thoughts overwhelming.
From the dying candle, the trembling smoke
Mixes its acrid odor with the plainchant singing.

From baptism to death, life is condensed
In this bland fragrance rising to the ceiling.
Reflecting on life's connections and significance,
We find a mixture of sad and happy feelings,
From the yellowed candle and its trembling smoke.

L'ODEUR DES BOIS, EN AUTOMNE

De son sabot, le cerf, grattant la feuille morte,
Fait monter des halliers une troublante odeur.
Odeur indéfinie, odeur ardente et forte,
Odeur de champignon, de fougère et de fleur.

Pour égarer des chiens la hurlante cohorte
Qui suit sous les grands bois son pas révélateur,
De son sabot, le cerf, grattant la feuille morte,
Fait monter des halliers une troublante odeur.

Des souvenirs fanés, hélas! Que nous importe
De voir s'éterniser la grisante douceur!...
Pour que le vent d'automne avec lui les emporte,
Par son souffle mêlant la peine et le bonheur,
Du passé, nous aussi, grattons la feuille morte.

THE SCENT OF THE WOODS IN AUTUMN

With its hoof, the deer scratches at the dead leaves,
Emitting a troubling scent from his wooded shelter.
Scent ardent, rich and borderless,
Scent of mushroom, fern and flower.

The howling dogs he attempts to mislead,
Who follow his revealing tracks through the timber.
With its hoof, the deer scratches at the dead leaves,
Emitting a troubling scent from his wooded shelter.

Faded memories, alas! It matters futilely
How long endures their intoxicating tenderness!...
Allow the winds of autumn to take them freely,
With a gust, combine pain and happiness,
Regarding the past, we, too, kick up dead leaves.

L'ENCENS

Dans les grains de l'encens se cache le mystère
Toujours inviolé des pays fabuleux;
Sur des charbons ardents son âme se libère
Et s'élève en flocons saints et voluptueux.

Du reflet des vitraux le soleil les éclaire,
Colorant leur néant de tons capricieux.
Dans les grains de l'encens se cache le mystère
Toujours inviolé des pays fabuleux.

C'est le parfum des dieux, l'hommage de la terre
Cherchant à dérider leurs fronts majestueux.
L'homme qui veut l'encens, dans sa gloire éphémère
Connaît l'âpre rancœur des déclins douloureux.
Dans les grains de l'encens se cache le mystère.

INCENSE

In the grains of incense lies hidden the mystery
Held sacrosanct by countries legendary;
By fiery coals, its soul is set free
And rises in clouds voluptuous and holy.

The sunlight reflecting through the windows glowingly,
Suffuses their nothingness with whimsical tones brightly.
In the grains of incense lies hidden the mystery
Held sacrosanct by countries legendary.

It is the perfume of the gods, earth's offering,
Seeking to unfurrow their brows sublime.
Man who seeks incense to his glory so fleeting
Will know the bitter rancor of his mortal decline.
In the grains of incense lies hidden the mystery.

LE FOIN COUPÉ

L'herbe n'a de parfum que lorsqu'elle est fanée
Et meurt dans les grands clos, à l'ombre des pommiers,
Lorsque la faux courbant sa tête profanée
A coups rythmés la couche au travers des sentiers.

Forêt qui n'a vécu que pendant une année,
Où l'insecte farouche a traqué son gibier,
L'herbe n'a de parfum que lorsqu'elle est fanée
Et meurt dans les grands clos, à l'ombre des pommiers.

O vous, obscurs soldats de la lutte acharnée
Herbe du champ français que va trancher l'acier,
De nos succès prochains, rançon prédestinée,
Songez, quand vous tombez en cueillant vos lauriers,
Que l'herbe n'a d'odeur que lorsqu'elle est fanée!
Rouen 1914

THE CUT HAY

Grass only has scent after the cutting,
As it dies under shady apple trees, in great mounds,
When the scythe, its profane head bending
In rhythmic strokes cuts it down.

A forest that was only a yearling,
Where their prey the wild insects would hound,
Grass only has scent after the cutting
As it dies under shady apple trees, in great mounds.

You are unknown soldiers in relentless endeavor,
Cut down by steel, the grass of French territory
For our future success, a predetermined expenditure.
Know, when you fall while earning your glory,
That grass only has scent after the cutting!
Rouen 1914

L'ODEUR EVAPORÉE

Dans le fond du cristal, l'odeur évaporée
De ses voiles légers se dévêt lentement
Et montre aux délicats son essence épurée
Que n'alourdissent plus d'importuns ornements.

Seuls les parfums exquis supportent la durée,
S'affaiblir n'est pour eux qu'un affranchissement.
Dans le fond du cristal, l'odeur évaporée
De ses voiles légers se dévêt lentement.

O femme aux blancs cheveux, aïeule vénérée,
Veilleuse du foyer qui s'éteint doucement
Par l'implacable doigt de la mort effleurée,
Sans que le cœur se trouble, on t'aspire ardemment
Dans le fond du cristal, odeur évaporée!

Pour Madame A…, Paris

THE EVAPORATED FRAGRANCE

At the bottom of the vial, the fragrance evaporated
Slowly undresses, its scent delicately apparent,
Revealing to the refined, its essence unadulterated
No longer weighed down by unwelcome embellishment.

Only the exquisite perfumes are never exhausted,
Evanescence, for them, represents emancipation.
At the bottom of the vial, the fragrance evaporated,
Slowly undresses, its scent delicately apparent.

O white-haired woman, ancestress venerated,
Light of the hearth, diminishing softly,
By death's relentless finger are you interrogated,
Without hesitation, we inhale your spirit ardently,
At the bottom of the vial, the fragrance evaporated.

For Madame A…, Paris

V

LES PETITES BÊTES
THE SMALL ANIMALS

LA CHOUETTE

La chouette est blottie au creux d'un arbre mort;
Sous son plumage gris son maigre corps frissonne,
Pendant que le soleil resplendit, elle dort.
Lorsqu'elle entr'ouvre un œil, tout la froisse et l'étonne:
Le coq, soudard brutal et mâle sans pudeur
Lance un appel strident sous sa crête vermeille;
Le chien, gardien farouche, éternel aboyeur
Répond à tous les bruits qui frappent son oreille;
L'homme, ce roi bavard et toujours agité
Semble avoir déclaré guerre au divin silence;
Ce ne sont que chansons, cris excès de gaîté,
Quand ce n'est pas colère ou scène de vengeance.
Le jour, fils du soleil règne en triomphateur
Sur les sillons brûlants, sur la poudreuse plaine,
Son pouvoir despotique engendre la torpeur
Etreint la volonté, la terrasse et l'enchaîne
Cependant peu à peu l'éclat du jour s'éteint:
Seul le haut peuplier perçant le crépuscule
Porte une lampe d'or sur un flambeau d'airain;
On dirait qu'à pas lents l'horizon se recule;
Sur l'homme se répand la dignité du soir,
En sa ruche de paille on voit rentrer l'abeille,
Le troupeau se rassemble et gagne l'abreuvoir,
Le monde est apaisé, l'oiseau des nuits s'éveille.

Une pâle clarté s'allume en ses yeux ronds
Dont les sourcils pointus s'élèvent en aigrette
Son aspect est rigide et son regard profond,
Son allure distante, imprécise et secrète.

Les détours arrondis d'un vol silencieux
L'amènent sur le haut d'un chêne solitaire;
Il demeure ébloui. L'attrait mystérieux

De la lune, élevant son blême lampadaire
Dans le ciel assombri: les limpides brouillards
Où l'étoile en tremblant met sa lueur bleuâtre.
La douceur des lointains, tout charme ses regards!
Il aime les combats du feu qui sort de l'âtre
Contre la brume, errant tout le long des marais
Pour tisser les draps blancs qui traînent sur les aulnes.
Dans ses brusques élans il suit le feu follet
Entraînant dans sa danse une troublante faune.

Pauvre oiseau méconnu! En cherchant l'idéal
Tu irrites les gens qui vivent dans la fange;
Ne te comprenant pas, le paysan brutal
Par les ailes te cloue aux portes de sa grange:
Être crucifié n'est-ce pas de tout temps
Le sort des incompris?.....Regarde à ma fenêtre
Il est quelqu'un là haut qui t'aime et qui ressent
Le charme sans éclat de ton âme champêtre.
Comme toi me ravit la calmante douceur
Des parfums de la nuit, l'apaisement de l'ombre.
J'admire comme toi la sublime grandeur
Des constellations brillant dans le ciel sombre;
J'aime à voir au reflet des couchants nébuleux
L'eau déployer les pans de sa robe de moire.....
Ne pouvant partager, ami, ton arbre creux
Je m'enferme, rêveur, dans une tour d'ivoire.
Grand-Couronne 1920

THE OWL

Snuggled in the hole of a dead tree
The owl, under its grey plumage, shivers.
It sleeps while the sun shines splendidly.
Upon half-opening an eye, everything annoys and astounds it:
The rooster, brutal ruffian, male without modesty,
Emits a strident call under its red aigrette;
The dog, fierce guardian, producer of cacophony,
Responds to every noise its ear detects;
Man, the loquacious king is always flighty
And seems to have declared war on divine silence;
With songs, shouts, excessive gaiety
Or scenes of rage or sounds of vengeance.
The day, son of the sun, reigns in domination
On the baking fields, on dusky plains,
His despotic power creates stagnation
Overcomes the will of the land it envelops and enchains.
Slowly but surely fades the day's scorch,
The top of the poplar pierces an evening cloudy
Carrying a golden lamp on a bronze torch;
It looks as if the horizon is shrinking languidly;
The dignity of the night descends on man's stature,
To its straw hive the bee retires,
The herd at the trough gather,
The world is calm, the night bird stirs.

A pale clarity in its round eyes expounds
With pointed eyebrows in tufts raised,
Its demeanor is stern, its stare profound,
Its look distant, secretive and ill-defined.

The circular detours of its silent avigation
Bring it to the top of an oak solitaire.
It remains dazzled by a mysterious fascination

Of the moon, lifting its pale flare
In the clouded sky; the transparent mist
Where trembling stars emit light azureous,
The faraway softness and all it can distinguish!
It enjoys from the hearth a fiery spectacle wondrous.
Against the mist, wandering in the marsh night
Weaving in the white sheets around the alders,
With swift movement, it follows the phosphorous light
Its dance startling wildlife explorers.

Poor misunderstood bird! In searching for the luminescent
You bother the people who live mired on the farm.
Misunderstanding you, the brutish peasant
Nails you by your wings to the doors of his barn.
Being crucified, is not that the fate
Of all the misunderstood?. . . Look to my window:
There is someone there who loves you and relates
To the simple charm of your country soul.
Like you I crave the tranquility,
The perfumes of the night, the shadows' density.
I admire, like you, the sublime majesty
Of the brilliant constellations in the dark sky;
I like to see the reflection in the twilight nebulous
Of the water spreading its silken attire.
Being unable to share, friend, your haven precious
I lock myself up, dreaming, in an ivory tower.
Grand-Couronne 1920

LE COQ

Libre, la crête en feu, gueux comme d'Artagnan,
Sur le fumier, le coq aime à chercher sa vie,
Et son cocorico annonce à tout venant
Qu'il tient vermisseau découvert pour sa mie.

Le manant étonné, trouve qu'il est plaisant
De travailler ainsi quand l'auge est bien garnie!
Libre, la crête en feu, gueux comme d'Artagnan,
Sur le fumier, le coq aime à chercher sa vie.

Philistins, mercantis, adipeux trafiquants,
Vous tous qui habitez la sage Béotie,
Qui pourrait faire entendre à vos esprits pesants
Qu'il n'est qu'un vrai bonheur: vivre à sa fantaisie,
Libre, la crête en feu, gueux comme d'Artagnan!
Bourbonne

THE ROOSTER

Free, comb of fire, a pauper like D'Artagnan,
On a mound of manure, the rooster explores his nature.
His crow announces in all directions
His hold on the worm captured for his lover.

This curious vagabond finds it amusing
To work so hard despite a trough full of treasure!
Free, comb of fire, a pauper like D'Artagnan
On a mound of manure, the rooster explores his nature.

Philistines, profiteers, corpulent traffickers,
All of you who live in wise Boeotia,
If only your ponderous souls could fathom
That there is only one true happiness: live your own utopia,
Free, comb of fire, a pauper like D'Artagnan!
Bourbonne

LE VIEUX CHIEN

Kosak, gardien fidèle, hirsute et chassieux,
Auprès de la maison, à l'ombre, aime à s'étendre.
C'est un vrai philosophe, il est las, il est vieux,
On voit le long du cou ses deux oreilles pendre.

Cependant, sur la route, un pas se fait entendre:
Brusquement éveillé, il ouvre les deux yeux.
Kosak, gardien fidèle, hirsute et chassieux,
Auprès de la maison, à l'ombre, aime à s'étendre.

Sourdement il aboie, hérissé et hargneux
On l'entend vers la porte en se traînant, se rendre.
Et puis il se recouche, au frais, silencieux;
Pour l'homme à la besace, il a un regard tendre
Kosak, gardien fidèle, hirsute et chassieux.
Ville-d'Avray 1911

THE OLD DOG

Kosak, faithful guardian, shaggy and rheumy,
Near the house, in the shade, loves to recline.
He is a true philosopher, aged and weary,
Along his neck his long ears droop in kind.

Meanwhile on the road, a step is heard, annoyingly:
Rudely awakened, he opens both eyes nearly blind.
Kosak, faithful guardian, shaggy and rheumy,
Near the house, in the shade, loves to recline.

Dully he barks, bristling and angry,
He drags himself to the door, then surrenders.
He lies back down, in the shade, quietly;
For the mailman he has feelings tender,
Kosak, faithful guardian, shaggy and rheumy.
Ville-d'Avray 1911

LE GRILLON

Chante, petit grillon, ta ronde monotone
Mon cœur est un enfant qu'il te plaît de bercer.
Les vents sont déchaînés, voici venir l'automne,
Reprends, fidèle ami, ta place à mon foyer.

Dans les jours de bonheur que le destin me donne
J'aime entendre, le soir, ton ronron familier.
Chante, petit grillon, ta ronde monotone
Mon cœur est un enfant qu'il te plaît de bercer.

Mais qu'adviennent les temps où tout l'être frissonne
Où, de son flot amer, sur nous vient déferler
La vague du malheur, où l'âme déraisonne:
Alors, pour m'apaiser, chante sans te lasser,
Chante, petit grillon, ta ronde monotone.

THE CRICKET

Sing, little cricket, your rhythmic melody.
My heart is a sleepy child you are rocking.
Here comes autumn with winds unleashed furiously,
Faithful friend, your place in my home is waiting.

In the days of joy that fate provides me
I enjoy hearing, at night, your familiar purring.
Sing, little cricket, your rhythmic melody,
My heart is a sleepy child you are rocking.

But when in time all the world shudders,
And upon us surges the floods bitter,
With wave of sorrow, our souls flustered,
Then soothe me, sing little cricket with vigor
Sing little cricket, your rhythmic melody.

LE MOINEAU

Le moineau, gai, pimpant, alerte et franc luron
Se conduit sans scrupule en parfait parasite.
Il est bruyant, hardi, vantard et fanfaron
Et se plaît à piller la maison qui l'abrite.

De bon cœur, le matin, l'ouvrière l'invite
A venir partager son repas sans façon.
Le moineau, gai, pimpant, alerte et franc luron
Se conduit sans scrupule en parfait parasite.

Vous ne lui voyez pas la mine déconfite
Quand le givre, au bois mort, donne des floraisons;
Au crottin, philosophe, il va rendre visite…
Ni disette, ni froid, n'arrêtent la chanson
Du moineau, gai, pimpant, alerte et franc luron.

THE SPARROW

The sparrow, dapper and genuinely joyful,
A perfect parasite with no compunction.
He is noisy, bold, a braggart, boastful,
He pillages the house that shelters him with elation.

The worker in the morning gives open invitation
To share her meal simple and cheerful.
The sparrow, dapper and genuinely joyful,
A perfect parasite with no compunction.

His countenance will not be troubled with fear
When the frost, on dead branches, blooms delicately.
Philosophically, on the dung pile he will appear…
No scarcity or cold stops the melody
Of the sparrow, gay, dapper, genuinely joyful.

LA TAUPE

Courte pattes, face têtue,
La taupe explore nos jardins
Coupant la tige de laitue
Que rencontre son souterrain.

Quand on la voit sur le chemin
On dirait qu'elle a la berlue…
Courte pattes, face têtue,
La taupe explore nos jardins.

Comme la bête noir vêtue
Nous poursuivons notre destin,
Allant à dia, allant à hue,
Et marchant d'un pas incertain,
Courtes pattes, face têtue…..

Ville-d'Avray

THE MOLE

Short legs, stubborn face,
The mole explores our gardens,
Cutting the stems of the lettuce
Encountered in its world hidden.

Seen on the trail it is out of place
It seems delusional and uncertain…
Short legs, stubborn face
The mole explores our gardens.

Like the animal dressed in black
We follow our destiny.
Moving this way and that
With steps unsure and hazy,
Short legs, stubborn face…

Ville-d'Avray

(Au Palais de Justice de Rouen, le vieux sculpteur
a mis sur les feuilles d'acanthe un escargot symbolique.)

L'ESCARGOT

Cul-de-jatte lourdaud, malfaisant et visqueux
L'escargot salit tout de sa bave argentée;
Promeneur inlassé, dès l'aube il est heureux
De cueillir sur la fleur la tremblante rosée.

Il passe sans remords, calme, majestueux,
Il a souillé la fleur, l'herbe est déshonorée.
Cul-de-jatte lourdaud, malfaisant et visqueux
L'escargot salit tout de sa bave argentée.

Dame Justice, hélas! d'allure est peu pressée;
Elle pose partout son large pied boueux.
Aussi le vieux sculpteur, en sa verve amusée,
A-t-il mis sur nos murs cet emblème fâcheux:
L'escargot, touche-à-tout, malfaisant et visqueux!

*(At the Palace of Justice in Rouen, the old sculptor
placed, on the acanthus leaves, a symbolic snail.)*

THE SNAIL

Legless, clumsy, evil, and slimy
The snail, with its silver spittle, dirties everything.
Tireless traveler at dawn, he is happy.
Picking at the dew, he leaves the flowers trembling.

He passes without remorse, calm and stately.
He dishonors the grass, the flowers defiling.
Legless, clumsy, evil, and slimy
The snail, with its silver spittle, dirties everything.

Lady Justice, alas! Not known for her celerity
Plants her large, muddy foot all over.
Therefore, the old sculptor, with amused energy,
Put on our walls this unflattering marker:
The snail touches all, evil and slimy!

LE MERLE

Le merle du jardin, vrai pitre en habite noir,
Croque-mort en goguette, est un pince-sans-rire,
Il court de ci, de là, et du matin au soir,
Des embûches du chat, avec honneur, se tire.

Les nerfs à fleur de peau, il saute, tourne, vire;
Escalade un râteau, inspecte un arrosoir,
Le merle du jardin, vrai pitre en habite noir,
Croque-mort en goguette, est un pince-sans-rire.

Mais quand le printemps naît, quand approche le soir,
Sublime, il rend hommage à l'amour qui l'inspire,
Célébrant tour à tour l'heure et le désespoir
Il trouve en son gosier les accents de Shakespeare,
Le merle du jardin, ce pitre en habit noir!...

THE BLACKBIRD

The blackbird of the garden, clown in black,
With deadpan expression, is like a merry undertaker,
Who runs from morning to night, this way and that,
And from the cat's ambush escapes with honor.

With nerves on edge, he jumps, turns and tacks,
Climbs a rake, gives a watering can the once over.
The blackbird of the garden, clown in black,
With deadpan expression, is like a merry undertaker.

But with springtime and evening's emanation
Inspired by love, sublimely, he gives tribute,
Celebrating alternately good fortune and desperation,
In his throat he finds Shakespearean attributes,
The blackbird of the garden, clown in black!

LES MOUSTIQUES

Le diable emporte le moustique
Cruel fléau de la saison!
Qui sous prétexte de musique,
Fait résonner un diapason.

Cet apache, au bon endroit, pique
Son surin à démangeaison;
Le diable emporte le moustique
Cruel fléau de la saison!

Souvent il vient dans nos maisons,
Des gens à semblables pratiques;
Quant au cœur est mis leur poison
Ils s'en vont en faisant la nique…
Le diable emporte ces moustiques!

MOSQUITOES

The devil brings the mosquito,
Cruel scourge of the season,
Who, under the pretext of a concerto,
Creates a tuning fork's resonation.

This Apache, with precision, strikes a blow
His arrow causes irritation;
The devil brings the mosquito,
Cruel scourge of the season!

Often they enter our habitation
People of a similar persuasion;
In the heart they place their corruption
Then leave, after making their impression…
The devil brings these mosquitoes!

LES FOURMIS

Cette république de nègres,
De nègres amis du labeur,
Dresse ses sujets peu intègres
Au métier de cambrioleur.

Que la chère soit bonne ou maigre,
Toujours elle y va de bon cœur
Cette république de nègres,
De nègres amis du labeur.

Là, point de princes ni de pègre,
Il n'y a que des travailleurs
Qui rapinent d'un pas allègre.
A-t-elle trouve le bonheur
Cette république de nègres?...

THE ANTS

This army of ebony
Of black admirers of exertion.
Its subjects trained masterfully
In the burglary profession.

The prize may be meager or plenty,
They always venture forth with elation,
This army of ebony,
Of black admirers of exertion.

There, neither criminals nor royalty,
There exists only the laborer
Who aggressively pillages, joyfully.
Did they find the answer
This army of ebony?...

LE HÉRISSON

Ce petit sanglier des bois lilliputiens
Quand il sent un danger sur lui-même se roule;
Il peut braver ainsi la morsure des chiens
Et le péril passé, indemne, se déroule.

Il sait que l'océan s'apaise après la houle,
Et qu'après l'ouragan, le ciel devient serein.
Ce petit sanglier des bois lilliputiens
Quand il sent le danger, sur lui-même se roule.

Le sage, aussi, se rit des noirceurs du destin;
Comme le hérisson, il met son cœur en boule,
Disant: «Il fait mauvais…il fera beau demain!»
Il est bon d'imiter, méprisé de la foule,
Le petit sanglier des bois lilliputiens.
Ville-d'Avray

THE HEDGEHOG

This little boar of the Lilliputian forest
Envelops himself when menace is discerned,
Thereby withstanding the dogs that molest,
Surviving the danger, he is unconcerned.

He knows the ocean subsides after tempest
After the storm, clear skies return.
This little boar of the Lilliputian forest
Envelops himself when menace is discerned.

The philosopher, also, laughs at tribulation,
Like the hedgehog, he protects his heart, saying
"Today is difficult but tomorrow will be outstanding!"
We should imitate him, though he is a vexation,
This little boar of the Lilliputian forest.
Ville-d'Avray

HOTES DES TOITS

Parmi les toits, pointus, les plinthes, les corniches,
Babille, aime et s'ébat le peuple des oiseaux.
Sous un chevron branlant l'hirondelle se niche,
Tous les trous du vieux mur abritent les moineaux.

Le pinson bon vivant à chacun fait des niches,
Pendant que le chat-huant boude au bord d'un chéneau.
Parmi les toits, pointus, les plinthes, les corniches,
Babille, aime et s'ébat le peuple des oiseaux.

La pie, en demi-deuil, de ses cris n'est pas chiche
Et trouble le pigeon, doux joueur de pipeaux.
Comme de liberté, d'amour, leur cœur est riche,
Tous ces êtres charmants s'épanouissent là-haut
Parmi les toits pointus, les plinthes, les corniches.
Bourbonne 1913

ROOFTOP GUESTS

All along the gables, columns, and pointed roofs
The birds twitter, love, rise and fall.
Under the rickety rafters, the swallows roost,
The sparrows fill all the holes in the old wall.

The bon-vivant finch with everyone goofs
While the screech owl broods above all.
Among the gables, columns, and pointed roofs
The birds twitter, love, rise and fall.

The magpie, in half-mourning, generous with its cries
Troubles the pigeons, chanting in soft prayer.
As with liberty and love, their vitality energizes,
These charming creatures all flourish up there,
Among the gables, columns, and pointed roofs.
Bourbonne 1913

HOTES DES CAVES

Au sous-sol ont logis les rats, les araignées,
Ne payant pas loyer, ces gens vivent heureux,
Dédaignant le confort, ils logent en chambrées
Et dans le coin choisi, s'installent deux par deux.

Les rats font dans la nuit de grandes randonnées,
Explorant les ruisseaux et les égouts fangeux.
Au sous-sol ont logis les rats, les araignées,
Ne payant pas loyer, ces gens vivent heureux.

Plus bourgeoise, Arachné mène une vie rangée,
File sans se lasser; mais ses instincts grincheux
Lui font prendre la mouche. Elle court, empressée,
Tout le long de son fil, puis…s'arrête au milieu.
Au sous-sol ont logis les rats, les araignées.

CELLAR GUESTS

In the basement the rats and spiders live,
They are content, paying rent they repudiate.
Disdaining comfort, they lodge, collaborative
And in their chosen corners, they conjugate.

The rats at night take long hikes, restive,
Exploring streams and sewers that stagnate.
In the basement the rats and spiders live,
They are content, paying rent they repudiate.

More bourgeois, Arachne, is more deliberative.
Spinning tirelessly, killer instinct at play
Enables her to catch her prey. She is attentive
And runs along her thread, then… stops halfway.
In the basement the rats and the spiders live.

LE POISSON ROUGE

Drapé dans sa robe écarlate
Que rehaussent des galons d'or
Prunelle ronde, échine plate
Le cyprin, sur l'eau trouble, dort.

Il songe aux jardins de la Chine,
A l'air grave du mandarin,
Et à vous, princesse mutine,
Souriant dans un palanquin.

Qui donc, parmi la troupe sombre
Des poissons, serait son rival?
Il a, soleil entouré d'ombre,
La dignité d'un cardinal.

Venu parfois à la surface
Pour goûter la saveur de l'air,
Il s'enfuit, faisant la grimace,
Et dit: «L'homme a des goûts pervers».

Lorsque le soleil, son complice,
Le caresse sous le jet d'eau,
Il allume un feu d'artifice
Sur les écailles de son dos.

S'il aime à ramper dans la fange,
Ce n'est certes pas surprenant.
L'homme peut-il trouver étrange
Ce qu'il fait lui-même souvent?

Un rustre passe et le contemple:
«Voilà, fait-il, un beau seigneur!
On dirait le suisse du temple
Menant à la chaire un recteur.

Mais passez-le dans la friture
Ce gentilhomme si parfait,
Il fera bien triste figure
Entre la carpe et le brochet!

L'habit jamais ne fit le moine
Et couleur n'est rien sans saveur:
Le bénéfice du chanoine
Vaut mieux que ses habits de chœur!»

Ainsi parle dans sa logique
L'homme guidé par la raison,
Et dont la flamme poétique
N'illumine pas l'horizon.
La nature a double visage
Comme Janus, le bi-fronté,
On voit, selon qu'on l'envisage,
L'utilité ou la beauté.

Il faut chevaucher Rossinante
Ou l'âne de Sancho Pança…
Dans leur sagesse décevante
Laissons ceux que n'émeuvent pas
La colline, à l'aube, empourprée,
L'heure que sonne le coucou
Blotti là-bas dans la hêtrée,
Les sonnailles chantant au cou
Des chevaux aux colliers de laine,
Le vent qui souffle sur les pins,
Et dans la paix de la fontaine,
Ce bijou vivant, le cyprin.

Grand-Couronne 1920

THE GOLDFISH

Draped in his scarlet cape
Which the golden stripes accentuate,
Inky round oculus, flat hard spine
The goldfish sleeps, even in troubled time.

He is daydreaming about the Chinese gardens,
Of the seriousness of the mandarin,
And of you rebellious princesses ardent
Smiling in a palanquin.

Who then among the dark tableau
Of the fish would be his rival?
The sunshine surrounded by shadow,
He has the dignity of a cardinal.

To the surface at times emerging
To taste the air's flavor,
He darts off, grimacing
Saying, "Man has strange behavior."

While the sun, his accomplice,
Through the water caresses
And ignites a firework chorus
On the scales of his back to impress.

If he enjoys crawling in the mire
This should not be viewed surprisingly.
Can man find beyond design
What he himself does frequently?

A peasant passes and observes admiringly:
"Look," he said, "What a noble demeanor!"
Verily this is royalty
Leading to the pulpit the rector.

But put it in a frying pan
This gentleman so perfect and right
And he will become a tragic man
Between the carp and the pike!

The garment never the monk defines
And color is nothing without flavor:
The wealth of the clergyman shines
And outweighs his clothing's nature!"

Thus speaks in logic
Man guided by reason
Whose poetic flame melodic
Does not illuminate the horizon.
Nature has a duality,
Like Janus, two-faced deity,
So we see, dependent on how we assay,
Utility or beauty.

Rocinante we must ride
Or Sancho Panza's donkey…
In their deceptive wisdom allied
Let us leave those with no empathy,
For the hills at dawn, purple rosy,
The hour at which the cuckoo sounds
Nestled in the beech tree,
The bells singing hanging down
From the horse's woolen collars,
The wind blowing through the pines,
And in the peace of the fountain gather,
The goldfish, this living jewel sublime.

Grand-Couronne 1920

VI

LES SONORITÉS
SOUNDS

L'OREILLE

Oreille, dans tes oubliettes
Est retenu captif le corps ailé des sons:
Troupe immense aux âmes fluettes
Qui monte en frémissant, se heurte et se confond.

Aveux, paroles indiscrètes
Il te faut tout subir, louanges et affronts.
Oreille, dans tes oubliettes
Est retenu captif le corps ailé des sons.

Le gai refrain des alouettes,
La musique, un baiser, la foudre, le canon,
Le bruissement des baïonnettes,
Le vent triste au soir, tout se perd et se fond
Oreille, dans tes oubliettes!....

THE EAR

Ear, in your dungeon stronghold
The wings of sound are held captive:
A large assembly of whispering souls
That rise, quivering, collide and merge reactive.

Confessions, words indiscreet and bold
You must endure all praise and insults subjective.
Ear, in your dungeon stronghold
The wings of sound are held captive.

The joyful refrain of the alouettes
A kiss, lightning, the cannon, melody,
The rattling of the bayonets,
All blend and become lost eventually
Ear, in your dungeon stronghold!...

LES HEURES SONNENT DANS LA NUIT

Tout bruit s'est apaisé depuis la fin du jour,
Tout s'est évanoui dans le silence et l'ombre;
Seuls les clochers pointus, les hauts pignons, les tours,
Se dressent imprécis, tout bleus dans le ciel sombre.
Jaloux de sa beauté les nuages sournois
Tendent leurs voiles blancs sous les pas de la lune
Qui voudrait se mirer dans l'ardoise des toits.
Le sommeil a chassé la haine et la rancune
Loin du cœur des humains. Intègre et méfiant
Dans le fond de sa niche, un chien tire sa chaîne
Contre le bois sonore, et se lève en grondant.
La brise aux foins séchés parfume son haleine
Et donne une caresse aux arbres exaltés
Par les ardeurs du jour; la nuit silencieuse
Règne dans la douceur et la sérénité.

Soudain s'élève au loin la voix mystérieuse
Des cloches, annonçant la mort de l'heure, entrant
Dans l'effroyable gouffre où tombent les années:
L'immensité sans borne et sans commencement.
Des voix flottent dans l'air, semences égrenées
D'une plante invisible et d'un arbre inconnu:
Sombre voix des bourdons, orgueil des cathédrales,
Voix frêles des couvents aux accents ingénus,
Qui donnent à regret leurs notes virginales;
Voix blanche et sans chaleur des cadrans officiels,
Voix où frémit toujours l'angoisse des tocsins;
Ces voix s'entremêlant s'élancent vers le ciel
En laissant un frisson dans les cloches d'airain.

La cathédrale est grave et son heure à pas lourds
Passe comme un chanoine en chape de velours;
Ses quarts, enfants de chœur au rochet de dentelle

Lestes et délurés gambadent devant elle.

    Saint Patrice un boitant
    Sur ses notes sautille
    Comme un blessé, marchant
    Courbé sur sa béquille.

Au bruit de la ferraille en vos décors pompeux,
Signes du zodiaque aux dessins fabuleux,
Le mouton du Beffroi, lentement se promène,
Symbole humiliant de la faiblesse humaine.
Tant de coups ont frappé depuis l'an treize cent
Sur la cache-ribaud, sur la cloche d'argent,
Qu'elles annoncent l'heure avec la fantaisie
De matrones ayant le mépris de la vie;
Elles disent: pourquoi d'une juste balance
Peser le temps qui court avec intransigeance?
La minute d'ennui s'écoule lentement
Mais les jours de bonheur ne durent qu'un moment.
Plein de mépris, Saint Ouen voit le cadran solaire
Dans son jardin, marquer une heure imaginaire
Sous les feux de la lune! Impeccable mentor
Il sonne l'heure exacte en redresseur de torts.
L'horloge du Palais, au fond de sa tourelle
Pleure d'avoir sonné le glas de la Pucelle!....

Tous ces chants peu à peu s'éloignent lentement
Leur vol harmonieux s'élargit et s'efface
Comme un brouillard léger sous le souffle du vent,
Comme l'ombre qui suit le nuage qui passe.
Le chien reprend son somme et l'homme épouvanté
Songe au temps qui poursuit sa course aventureuse.
La nuit, dans la douceur et la sérénité
Sur la ville s'étend, calme et silencieuse....

                Rouen, Août 1917

THE HOURS RINGING IN THE NIGHT

All noise abates by end of day,
All fades in silence and obscurity;
Only the pointed steeples and towers stay,
Against the somber sky, rising indistinctly.
The furtive clouds, jealous of their beauty
Under the moon stretch their white veils,
Wishing to reflect on the slate roofs admiringly.
Hatred and rancor sleep has assailed,
Human hearts can rest. Secure and suspicious
Within his nook, a dog pulls on his chain
Against the creaking wood, rises and growls officious.
The breeze of dry hay perfumes his domain,
And gives a caress to noble trees
After the day's passion; the night reigns
In silent softness and serenity.

Suddenly from afar rises a mysterious cry
Of bells announcing the death of the hour which descends
Into the frightful chasm falls time:
Boundless and beginningless immensity.
Voices float in air, seeds combine
From the invisible plant and unknown tree:
The bells' somber voices, pride of the monastery,
Frail voices from the convent with innocent esprit
Their virginal notes given reluctantly;
The clocks' cold official voices without empathy,
Voices that shudder with anguish and urgency,
These voices mingled, launching toward eternity
Reverberating in the bronze bells.

The cathedral is somber, its hour is late
Passing like a bishop in velour cape,
Its quarter hours like choirboys in lace

Leaping, light-footed, frolic with grace.

>Saint Patrick limping along
>His thoughts skipping
>Like a wounded man, walking
>Over his cane, bending.

Amidst the metal clang, in its pompous placement,
Zodiac signs in beautiful arrangement,
The lamb of the Belfry saunters lazily
Humbling symbol of human frailty.
So many blows struck since the year thirteen hundred
On the evening bell and silver clock resplendent.
They announce the hour so seriously
Like officious old matrons who view life scornfully;
They say: why such a struggle
To measure time so inflexibly?
A minute of worry passes slowly
But days of joy past instantly.
With indifference, Saint-Ouen views the sundial tower
In its garden, marking an imaginary hour.
Under the moonlight! Exemplary mentor,
It announces the exact hour to right all error.
The clock of the Hall of Justice at the bottom of its turret,
Having struck the Maid's death knell, cries in regret! ....

All these songs slowly dissipate
Their harmonious journey widens and clears,
Like a light fog under a breath of wind evaporates
Like a shadow that disappears.
The dog resumes its nap, and man with anxiety
Contemplates Time, which continues its adventurous journey.
The night in softness and serenity
Envelopes the town, calmly and quietly….

Rouen, August 1917

LE VENT CHANTE DANS LES FILS TÉLÉGRAPHIQUES

Quel est ce chant suave à la tendre harmonie
Léger comme un parfum que dissipe le vent?
Quelle âme peut trouver dans sa mélancolie
La troublante langueur de ces tristes accents?

Les prosaïques fils de la télégraphie,
Juchés sur leurs grands mâts, nous montrent l'instrument
D'où vient ce chant suave à la tendre harmonie
Léger comme un parfum que dissipe le vent.

N'écoutons pas les gens parlant philosophie,
Ils prônent la raison et nous le sentiment.
Que m'importe le fil chantant la mélodie!
J'écoute le concert sans chercher autrement
D'où vient l'hymne suave à la tendre harmonie.

Saint-Valery 1918

WIND SINGING IN THE TELEGRAPH WIRES

What is this sweet song of tender harmony
Light as perfume floating on the breeze?
What soul cannot find in its melancholy
A troubling languor in its sad reprise?

Telegraph lines so ordinary,
Perched on high, show us the keys
Where comes this elegant song of tender harmony,
Light as perfume floating on the breeze.

Listen not to those who speak philosophically,
They advocate reason, but we, feeling.
I care not which wire sings such melody!
I listen to the concert without caring
Where comes this sweet hymn of tender harmony
Saint-Valery 1918

LE BRUIT DE LA FORGE

Le forgeron velu frappe à coups cadencés
Sur le métal sonore, au reflet rose tendre;
Le fer, ce roi du monde, honteux et convulsé,
Sort, tout vibrant du feu, comme la salamandre.

La forge a son chant grave au rythme balancé
Dont le charme est profond lorsqu'on sait le comprendre.
Le forgeron velu frappe à coups cadencés
Sur le métal sonore, au reflet rose tendre.

Le lourd soufflet gémit; par les poids abaissés
Ses cercles de bois roux se mettent à descendre;
Et ses poumons de cuir, de leur souffle oppressé,
Font crépiter le feu qui dormait sous la cendre…
Le forgeron velu frappe à coups cadencés.
Bourbonne

THE SOUND OF THE FORGE

The hirsute blacksmith strikes in cadence
On the ringing metal with roseate appearance,
Iron, king of the world, beaten without reverence
Emerges, like the salamander, with brilliant vibrance.

The forge sings softly in balanced rhythm
And if understood, has profound wisdom.
The hirsute blacksmith strikes in cadence
On the ringing metal with roseate appearance.

The heavy bellow groans; with weight as guidance
The red wooden paddles begin their descent,
From suppressed exhalation, the lungs of leather
Awaken the ashes and the fire augments.
The hirsute blacksmith strikes in cadence.
Bourbonne

LE CHANT DE LA CLOCHE

*Le son se détachant de la cloche ébranlée
Tombe comme un fruit mûr, très lourd et savoureux.
Par ses coups répètes, l'oreille martelée
Goûte l'âpre douceur d'un plaisir douloureux.*

*Le chant gagne les bois et couvre la vallée
D'un filet invisible aux rêts mystérieux…
Le son se détachant de la cloche ébranlée
Tombe comme un fruit mûr, très lourd et savoureux.*

*Mais voilà que des vents, la troupe échevelée
Suspend du chant sacré le cours majestueux,
L'éloigne, le ramène en sa rage affolée,
Et parait élever, pantelant, jusqu'aux cieux,
Le son se détachant de la cloche ébranlée.*

THE SONG OF THE BELL

The struck bell emits the melody
That falls like ripe fruit, heavy and savory.
By repetitive strokes the ear pressured,
Tastes the sweetness of painful pleasure.
The song reaches the woods and covers the valley
In an invisible net of mysterious conspiracy…
The struck bell emits the melody
That falls like ripe fruit, heavy and savory.
The winds arrive in force and expel
The sacred song with its majestic purport,
Separates and recaptures in agitated swells,
Elevating, breathlessly, to the sky it transports,
The melody of the struck bell.

LE CHANT DU CRAPAUD

La laideur du crapaud rend sa chanson plus belle,
Venant d'un tel gosier, sa douceur nous surprend;
Note unique au son pur, plainte immatérielle
Exhalant les désirs de l'âme des étangs,

On dirait qu'échappant à l'étreinte charnelle
Vers le ciel désiré vous prenez votre élan!
La laideur du crapaud rend sa chanson plus belle,
Venant d'un tel gosier, sa douceur nous surprend.

Le silex en ses flancs renferme l'étincelle,
Sur son cœur le vieillard aime à presser l'enfant,
Dans notre corps fangeux chante une âme immortelle,
L'ombre donne au soleil un éclat plus brillant,
La laideur du crapaud rend sa chanson plus belle!

THE SONG OF THE TOAD

The toad's ugliness beautifies its descant,
The sweetness from such a throat surprises.
A unique note of pure tone, a spiritual lament;
The desires of the pond's soul it comprises.

From its fleshy embrace it escapes, transcendent
Toward the sky, with desire it rises!
The toad's ugliness beautifies its descant,
The sweetness from such a throat surprises.

The flint encases the spark luminescent,
The old man embraces the child with passion,
In our miry body sings an immortal song extant,
The shade gives the sun a more brilliant radiation,
The toad's ugliness beautifies its descant!

LES CHIENS ABOIENT DANS LA NUIT

*On entend s'élever des profondeurs obscures
De la perfide nuit, l'aboi rauque des chiens,
Gardant d'un cœur égal les palais, les masures,
Le toit du prolétaire ou du patricien.*

*Ecartant les rôdeurs aux troublantes allures,
Sans l'espoir d'un merci, ardent, ne craignant rien,
On entend s'élever des profondeurs obscures
De la perfide nuit, l'aboi rauque des chiens.*

*Cette voix, menaçant de cruelles morsures
L'envahisseur sournois des logis mitoyens,
C'est la voix de dieu Pan, protecteur des cultures,
C'est l'éternel appel du devoir et du bien
Qu'on entend s'élever des profondeurs obscures.*

DOGS BARKING IN THE NIGHT

We hear rising from the depths dim and hazy
The dogs' hoarse bark, in the night perfidious and black,
Protecting with equal passion palaces or shanties,
Homes of proletariat or aristocracy.

Scattering the prowlers menacing and wary
With no need for gratitude, fearless on the attack.
We hear rising from the depths dim and hazy
The dogs' hoarse bark, in the night perfidious and black.

From cruel jaws, that voice threatens and bullies
The sneaky invader entering neighboring sites,
It is the voice of the god Pan, protector of shepherds and
    country,
It is the eternal call of duty and what is right
That we hear rising from the depths dim and hazy.

LE CHANT DES GOUTTES D'EAU

*Chaque goutte qui tombe a un son différent
Et donne à sa chanson sa note personnelle.
Le chant des gouttes d'eau, narquois et sautillant
Semble parfois l'écho de quelque villanelle.*

*Au fond du vase obscur on dirait qu'on entend
D'un violon lointain vibrer la chanterelle.
Chaque goutte qui tombe a un son différent
Et donne à sa chanson sa note personnelle.*

*Parfois sa voix est grave, austère, solennelle,
Puis brusquement éclate en un rire d'enfant,
Le mystère insondé, c'est que rien ne décèle
Pourquoi du même endroit au même point chutant
Chaque goutte qui tombe a un son différent.*

THE SONG OF WATERDROPS

Each drop that falls has a different harmony
And gives the song its personal artistry.
The drops of water mocking, hopping musically,
Resemble at times the echo of poetry.

At the bottom of the vase we hear obscurely
A distant violin's vibrating melody.
Each drop that falls has a different harmony
And gives the song its personal artistry.

At times, its voice is serious, solemn, surly,
Then abruptly bursts in childish laughter and shouts.
It cannot be resolved, an unsolved mystery,
Why from the same spot, the same spout
Each drop that falls has a different harmony.

VIOLON ET VIOLONCELLE

Couchés nonchalamment sur le canapé rose
Grand frère et petit frère aiment à rêvasser ;
Mais sur le piano, dès que la main se pose,
On entend l'harmonique en leurs flancs résonner.

Leur âme est en émoi, et, curieuse chose,
Dès qu'ils sont éveillés, se mettent à ronfler.
Couchés nonchalamment sur le canapé rose
Grand frère et petit frère aiment à rêvasser.

Grand frère exhale un chant langoureux et morose
Petit frère, en fausset, se plait à gambader
Et sur un cri aigu, pour terminer, se pose…
Et puis, toujours d'accord, ils vont se reposer
Couchés nonchalamment sur le canapé rose.
Ville-d'Avray

VIOLIN AND CELLO

Reclined on the rose-colored sofa nonchalantly,
Big brother and little brother enjoy daydreaming.
But, when hands touch the piano, invariably
Their harmony from within begins resonating.

Their soul is stirring, and curiously,
As they awaken, they begin snoring.
Reclined on the rose-colored sofa nonchalantly,
Big brother and little brother enjoy daydreaming.

Big brother exhales, languid and morose,
Little brother's falsetto frolics happily,
And with a sharp cry, a close, grandiose…
And then together, they rest amicably,
Reclined on the rose-colored sofa nonchalantly.
Ville-d'Avray

LE VENT

Vent, qui es-tu? Dieu ou Démon
Toi dont la voix sans cesse clame,
Faut-il te mettre au Panthéon?
Est-ce l'enfer qui te réclame?

Sur le front soucieux des eaux,
C'est le vent qui creuse des rides,
Il fait peur au craintif oiseau:
Ce miroir brisé l'intimide!
En avril, vent, quand tu es doux,
Tu viens libérer les fontaines,
Sous bois on entend leurs glouglous,
Parmi les hêtres et les chênes.

    Vent, qui es-tu?...

Sous les efforts de l'ouragan,
La forêt s'incline, apeurée,
Le vieux cerf s'enfuit en bramant,
Croyant qu'on sonne la curée...
Les gosiers des oiseaux chanteurs
Te sont des harpes éoliennes,
Où tu te complais, quand berceur,
A nous jouer des cantilènes.

    Vent, qui es-tu?...

Tu veux des sublimes jouets,
Les jours d'orage et de rafales,
Terrible enfant dont les hochets
Sont les vieux coqs des cathédrales!
D'autres soirs, tu sais badiner,
Tu es courtois, galant, volage,

Il te convient de lutiner
Quelque boucle autour d'un visage.

    Vent, qui es-tu?...

Pourquoi voulais-tu enlever
A ce malheureux sa guenille?
Il a déjà peine à braver
Les assauts de dame la Pluie!
S'il te plaît de nous tourmenter,
Si ta violence nous alarme,
Pourquoi cherches-tu à sécher
Jusqu'à la trace de nos larmes?

    Vent, qui es-tu?...

Dans un logis, quand le feu prend,
Tu voudrais brûler la marmaille,
Et tu hurles: c'est le grand vent
Qui détruit tout, vaille que vaille!
Sur les terrasses d'Orient,
On t'appelle la Brise aimée
Qui met son charme caressant
Dans les grands yeux noirs des almées

    Vent, qui es-tu?...

Pour certains, tu es un grand dieu,
Quand tu t'élèves, tout s'abaisse;
Au loin s'enténèbrent les cieux,
Toute force devient faiblesse.
Peut-être aussi, quand incompris
Serais-tu fait des âmes lasses
D'errer autour du Paradis
Et qui doivent y trouver place;
Ou bien, ce qui serait trop haut

Pour que notre âme s'y apaise,
Cet esprit voguant sur les eaux
Au temps lointain de la Genèse?

Vent, qui es-tu?...

WIND

Wind, who are you? God or Devil
You with voice unrelenting,
Should you be honored in the Pantheon as special?
Is hell demanding a reclaiming?

On the water's worried surface,
It's the wind that carves wrinkles.
The fearful birds are scared wordless
By this broken mirror's ripples!

In April, wind, when you are gentle,
The springs you come to liberate
Deep in the woods we hear their trickle
Among the beeches, oaks and dates.

      Wind, who are you?

From the storm's undertaking,
The forest bends in distress.
The old stag flees, bellowing,
Believing the hunt is in progress…
The full-throated calls of songbirds on high
To you, Aeolian harps they portray.
Or are you happiest with lullabies?
For us, some cantilenas you will play.

      Wind, who are you?

You want to play and battle
During days of rage and upheaval,
Terrible child whose rattles
Are weathervanes on steeples!
Other nights you prefer to banter
You display courtesy, gallantry, grace.

It pleases you to tease and tamper
With a few curls around a face.

    Wind, who are you?

Why would you remove and tear
From that unfortunate his cane?
He already has much abuse to bear
From the assaults of Lady Rain!
If it pleases you to torment on high,
If your violence alarms and terrifies,
Why do you seek to dry
So completely the tears from our eyes?

    Wind, who are you?

At home when the fire alights,
You try to burn the children in the hall,
You shout, it's the great wind that bites
And destroys everything after all!
On the terraces of the Orient,
They call you Wind Divine,
Who creates caressing charms of content
In the dark eyes of lovers entwined.

    Wind, who are you?

For some, a great god harkens.
When you rise, all stoop and quail;
In the far distance, skies darken,
All power becomes frail.
Maybe, too, misunderstood mysteriously,
Might you be comprised of the weary souls,
Who in Paradise wander aimlessly,
Searching for meaning, wanting to be whole;
Or perhaps you are above understanding

Unable to help our souls find solace,
This spirit blown across the waters meandering
Since the faraway time of Genesis?

Wind, who are you?

VII

LES RÊVERIES

DREAMS

LA PEPITE D'OR

L'humble pépite d'or chemine au fond des eaux
Parant d'un fauve éclat les limons et les sables:
Dans son isolement, ce n'est qu'un grain plus beau
Prïs dans le tourbillon d'autres grains innombrables.

Que d'efforts, que de soins pour en faire un lingot,
Pour former un joyau de sa poudre impalpable!
L'humble pépite d'or chemine au fond des eaux
Parant d'un fauve éclat les limons et les sables.

Notre bonheur, non plus, quoi qu'en pensent les sots,
N'est pas un plat qu'un jour on trouve sur la table;
Heureux qui sait grouper, choisir, mettre en faisceau
        Ses éléments impondérables,
Humble pépites d'or cheminant sous les eaux!
                    Paris.

THE GOLDEN NUGGET

The humble gold nugget shuffles downstream
Adorning silt and sand with fawn-colored radiance;
In its isolation, it is simply a grain that gleams
Caught in the whirlwind with grains miscellaneous.

Such effort and care, to make an ingot beam,
To form a jewel from its powder's brilliance!
The humble gold nugget shuffles downstream
Adorning silt and sand with fawn-colored radiance.

Our happiness, no less, whatever fools deem
Is not a plate we simply find on our table;
Happy are those who know how to sort and seam
        Its elements imponderable,
The humble gold nugget shuffles downstream!
                    Paris.

L'AVENIR, LE PRÉSENT, LE PASSÉ

L'avenir c'est l'oiseau qu'on chasse,
D'autant plus convoité qu'il est moins défini,
Qui vole dans laisser de trace
Et dont personne, hélas! ne découvre le nid.

L'oiseau tombe comme une masse,
C'est le présent brutal qui nait quand il finit;
L'avenir c'est l'oiseau qu'on chasse,
D'autant plus convoité qu'il est moins défini.

Seul le passé n'est pas fugace
Et se fixe dans l'infini,
Mais comme l'oiseau qu'on ramasse,
Le doigt de la mort l'a terni.
L'avenir c'est l'oiseau qu'on chasse. . . .

THE FUTURE, THE PRESENT, THE PAST

The future is the bird we chase,
All the more coveted, being less defined.
It flies without leaving a trace
With a nest, alas! we can never find.

Like a bird that falls heavily in haste,
The brutal present is born and left behind.
The future is the bird we chase,
All the more coveted, being less defined.

Only the past is not impermanent,
Forever fixed in the infinite.
But like a fallen bird unfortunate
The finger of death has tarnished it.
The future is the bird we chase…

LA CENDRE

Au repos, à l'oubli nous fait songer la cendre,
Cheveux blancs sur le front du feu qui va mourir,
Sur le rouge tison, linceul qui va s'étendre,
Désert glacé ou toute ardeur doit aboutir.

Vous êtes révolus, temps de la Salamandre,
Le bûcher du Phénix n'est plus qu'un souvenir;
Au repos, à l'oubli nous fait songer la cendre,
Cheveux blancs sur le front du feu qui va mourir.

Le cœur aussi s'éteint; la vieillesse est peu tendre,
La cendre du passé l'empêche de sentir…
Que de bonheurs perdus faute de les comprendre,
Mais aussi que de deuils supportés sans souffrir!
Au repos, à l'oubli nous fait songer la cendre.

ASHES

Observing the ashes, we muse on oblivion,
White-like hair on the brow of a dying fire,
On the red ember, a shroud has fallen,
A frozen desert, where all passion expires.

You have now passed, a fire downtrodden,
The Phoenix pyre, a memory prior.
Observing the ashes, we muse on oblivion,
White hair on the brow of a dying fire.

The heart also fades, old age is a toxin,
The ashes of the past hinder it from feeling…
How many joys lost due to misunderstanding,
But also lessens the sadness of suffering!
Observing the ashes, we muse on oblivion.

LES FEUILLES MORTES

Douce neige de pourpre et d'or,
Les feuilles tombent sur la terre;
Seul, le chêne hautain garde encor
Sa fauve parure éphémère.

Sous les assauts du vent du nord
S'amoncelle sur les bruyères
Douce neige de pourpre et d'or…
Les feuilles tombent sur la terre.

Triste, la nature s'endort
A l'approche de ce mystère
De l'hiver, qui, las, vient encor
Donner pour lit au pauvre hère
Douce neige de pourpre et d'or.
                    Versailles

THE DEAD LEAVES

Soft snow of crimson and gold,
The leaves fall to the ground;
Only the haughty oak still holds
It's tawny ephemeral crown.

By the north winds scold
Amassing on shrubs in mounds,
Soft snow of crimson and gold
The leaves fall to the ground.

Nature, saddened, falls asleep
With this approaching mystery
As winter wearily unfolds
A bed for the tired and unlucky
Of soft snow, crimson and gold.
                    Versailles

LA NUIT

L'amour et la douleur accompagnent la nuit,
Reine de volupté, déesse du mystère,
Douce amante du soir qui s'avance sans bruit
Quand le soleil lassé s'éloigne de la terre.

La lune aux yeux jaloux sans cesse la poursuit,
Et cherche à l'accabler de son éclat austère.
L'amour et la douleur accompagnent la nuit,
Reine de volupté, déesse du mystère.

Elle est douce: au cœur tendre elle offre son appui;
De maints propos charmants elle est la conseillère.
Elle est dure et féroce, alors qu'en son réduit
Obscur, elle a livré la pauvre à sa misère!
L'amour et la douleur accompagnent la nuit.

THE NIGHT

Love and sorrow accompany the night,
Sensual queen, goddess of mystery.
Evening's gentle lover approaching quietly,
As the sun fades from the earth wearily.

The moon with jealous eyes keeps her in sight,
Seeking to overwhelm her with his austere intensity.
Love and sorrow accompany the night,
Sensual queen, goddess of mystery.

Softly, to the tender heart she offers solace,
With guidance given to many charming inquiries.
Yet she is harsh and cruel, for in his plight,
She has left the poor man in his misery!
Love and sorrow accompany the night.

NOCES D'ARGENT

La barque vogue en paix vers la rive incertaine
Quand le pilote sait éviter les remous,
Et que la passagère, au bout de la carène,
Conduit le gouvernail d'un geste ferme et doux.

Accorder ses efforts, c'est la règle certaine
Pour n'être pas un jour brisés sur les cailloux.
La barque vogue en paix vers la rive incertaine
Quand le pilote sait éviter les remous.

Cet accord de deux cœurs dans l'affection sereine
Nous l'avons conservé avec un soin jaloux
Et depuis vingt-cinq ans, dans la joie et la peine,
Dans les déceptions, les chagrins, les à-coups,
La barque vogue en paix vers la rive incertaine.
7 Juin 1919

SILVER WEDDING ANNIVERSARY

A boat will sail peacefully along an uncertain shore
When the pilot knows how to avoid the eddies,
And the passenger in the stern, furthermore,
Controls the rudder smoothly and firmly.

Coordinating these efforts is an important chore,
The rocks pose an ongoing threat most deadly.
A boat will sail peacefully along an uncertain shore
When the pilot knows how to avoid the eddies.

This accord of two hearts in serene rapport
We have protected with vigilant care,
And so for twenty-five years, in joy and war,
With disappointments, sorrows, wear, and tear,
The boat sails peacefully along an uncertain shore.
June 7, 1919

L'HOMME ET LA FEUILLE

L'HOMME

Tombe, tombe, feuille dorée,
Quitte les bras du marronnier,
Tu verras, ce soir de rosée,
Que l'herbe est un doux oreiller.

LA FEUILLE

Pauvre homme! Suis ta destinée!
Tu tomberas un beau matin,
N'es-tu pas la feuille attachée
Sur le grand arbre du destin!

L'HOMME

Comme tu dois souffrir, tristement repliée
Le soir où la tempête hurle au sommet des monts!
Mais que j'aime à te voir, au soleil, dilatée,
Chanter avec la brise un hymne à Apollon.

LA FEUILLE

Entre nos deux destins, grande est la ressemblance,
Il faut de chauds rayons pour entr'ouvrir ton cœur;
Le froid, pour toi, s'appelle haine ou indifférence,
Le soleil de ton âme a pour nom le bonheur.

L'HOMME

La feuille en zig-zag tourbillonne
Et parfois attaque de front
La cohorte agile et brouillonne
Des moustiques dansant en rond.

LA FEUILLE

Ta conduite est-elle sensée
Alouette allant au miroir,
Quand tu laisses errer ta pensée
Dans un vol de papillons noirs?

L'HOMME
Au sortir du bourgeon, feuille, tu es jolie,
L'hiver par toi vaincu sourit en s'enfuyant;
Tu es plus belle encore, en ta robe jaunie,
Gai linceul dont la mort ennoblit ton néant.

LA FEUILLE
L'enfant est beau comme la feuille à sa naissance;
Mais, au soir de la vie, alors que tu t'éteins
Homme! la mort pour toi n'a pas la bienveillance
De voiler de beauté l'horreur de ton destin.

L'HOMME
Tes discours en font foi, feuille, tu es légère,
Les vents, tes, grands amis, sont pauvres conseillers,
C'est quand nous finissons qu'entre nous tout diffère:
Pour toujours tu t'endors, l'homme va s'éveiller.
Il ne restera rien de ta robe dorée,
Orgueil de ta vieillesse. Au fond d'un chemin creux
L'hiver la roulera, flétrie et déchirée;
Voilà quel est ton sort, et ton sort est affreux!
Pour nous, feuille, ma mie, a l'âme libérée,
S'ouvrent dans l'au-delà de vastes horizons!
Au déclin de tes jours finit ta destinée…
C'est lorsque nous mourons, feuille, que nous naissons!
                    Automne 1912

THE MAN AND THE LEAF

THE MAN
Fall, fall, golden leaf,
Leave the arms of the chestnut tree,
This dewy night you will find relief
On the grass, a pillow feathery.

THE LEAF
Poor man! Follow your destiny!
You will one fine morning, with certainty,
Fall like a leaf, attached only briefly
To the great tree of destiny!

THE MAN
How you must suffer, so sadly tossed
At night when the mountain storm hurls you about!
But how I love to see you, in the sun, aloft
Singing with the breeze to Apollo, a hymn so devout.

THE LEAF
How our two destinies are similar,
Warm rays are needed to open your heart;
Cold, for you, is considered hard and sinister,
Happiness is the sun for your spirit.

THE MAN
The leaf is caught in a whirl
And at times hits head-on and hurtles
The agile but addled swirl
Of mosquitoes dancing in circles.

THE LEAF
Your behavior, does it make sense,
A lark, flying into a mirror,
When you let your thoughts cause offense
In a moment of darkness and terror?

THE MAN

As you grow, leaf, you are lovely,
Winter you defeat, it smiles in its failure;
In your yellow gown you are even more comely,
A gay shroud that ennobles your departure.

THE LEAF

The child is as beautiful as the leaf at nativity,
But in the evening of life while you fade markedly,
Man! Death for you does not have the ability
To mask with beauty the horror of your destiny.

THE MAN

Such reasoning proves, leaf, you are a lightweight,
The winds, your friends, advise poorly for your sake,
It's at the end that we bifurcate:
You sleep forever, but man will awake.
Nothing will remain of your golden robe,
The pride of old age. At the bottom of a shallow road
Winter will dispatch you, withered and torn;
There is your end and how forlorn!
Whereas we, leaf my friend, await ecstasy,
Our souls released into a vast horizon, adorned!
The end of your days, ends your destiny…
However, when we die, leaf, we are reborn!

Autumn 1912

LE VIEUX SECRÉTAIRE

Le vieux secrétaire ventru
De palissandre et bois de rose,
Dans le grenier, loin des intrus,
Depuis près d'un siècle repose.
Peu à peu le temps a terni
Ses ferrures, ses charnières;
Sur son placage déverni
Dorment de lourdes poussières.
La main qui ferma ses tiroirs
Pleins de reliques, est glacée:
Dans le passé aux voiles noirs,
Son image s'est effacée.
C'est le tombeau des souvenirs,
Le trait d'union qui relie
Les petits enfants à venir
A toute une race abolie.
C'est le modeste confident
Des doux émois de la tendresse
Dans les jours de déchirement
Et les courts instants d'allégresse.
On entend le grignotement
Du ver, qui ronge sans relâche,
Symbolique émule du Temps
Que rien n'arrête dans sa tâche.
Par des craquements furieux
Le bois clame sa déchéance,
On dirait l'appel douloureux
Du noble instinct de survivance.

. . . .

Les rideaux sont fermés. Dans ses oreillers blancs,
Elle repose en paix, celle qui est partie. . .

Sur ses traits détendus règne un apaisement
Qui semble surtout fait du mépris de la vie.
    Un chapelet est enroulé
    A ses pauvres mains amaigries,
    Tout un passé s'est écroulé
    Qui gît là, entre deux bougies!

Dans un air confiné, le lourd parfum des fleurs
A l'arôme irritant de l'éther se mélange;
On sent rôder là-bas l'ange de la douleur,
Tout nous semble changé, tout nous paraît étrange.
    Cette affaire qu'hier encor
    Nous trouvions inquiétante,
    Devant la grandeur de la mort
    Est devenue indifférente.
    Dans une boîte, nous serrons
    Les fleurs qui se fanaient sur elle
    Et les cheveux que nous coupons
    Sous sa coiffure de dentelle.
    Nous enfermons dans la douceur
    De ces violettes de Parme,
    Tout un lambeau de notre cœur
    Et l'amertume d'une larme. . .
    Dans le secrétaire accueillant,
    Nous rangeons nos pauvres reliques
    Auprès des boîtes contenant
    Bien des souvenirs identiques.
    Ainsi se forgent les maillons
    Dont est faite la forte chaîne
    Guidant les générations
    Au cours de leur route incertaine.
                 Pour M. et G., Paris

THE OLD SECRETARY DESK

The pot-bellied old secretary desk
Of palisander and rosewood,
In the attic, far from intruders, statuesque,
For almost a century rests.
Little by little time has tarnished
Its locks, its hinges creaking;
On its veneer unvarnished
Dust lies heavily sleeping.
The hand that closed its drawers
Full of relics is now cold;
Through the mist of distant shores
An image we can no longer behold.
It is a tomb of memories,
A connection that links
The little children yet to be
To a complete generation gone in a wink.
It is the modest confidant
Of the sweet emotions of tenderness
During life's difficult days of want
With its brief moments of joy and gentleness.
We hear the nibbling
Of the worm, which gnaws tirelessly,
Symbolic imitator of Time working
Which toils relentlessly.
With furious cracking
The wood proclaims its degradation,
As if making a painful cry announcing
It's noble instinct of self-preservation.
....

The curtains are drawn. On her white pillows,
She rests in peace, she who has departed....

On her relaxed features tranquility follows,
A disdain for life seemingly imparted.

> A rosary is wound
> Around her poor thin hands.
> An entire history run aground
> Which lies there, between two candles!

In the confined air, the flowers' heavy perfume
With the aroma of ether is irritatingly interchanged;
The angel of sorrow's obtrusive presence looms
Everything feels changed, everything seems strange.

> The situation encountered yesterday
> That we found so worrisome and alarming,
> Confronted by the magnitude of death's decay
> Has become irrelevant and unbecoming.
> In a box we press sadly
> The flowers that fade upon her
> And the lock of hair we cut devotedly
> From under her lace headdress demure.
> We enclose in the softness
> Of these violets of Parme sincere,
> A piece of our heart, hapless,
> And the bitterness of a tear…

> In the desk welcoming,
> Our poor relics we keep
> With nearby boxes containing
> Similar souvenirs in heaps.
> Thus are created the bonds
> That forge a strong chain
> Guiding our scions
> Along their uncertain terrain.

For M. and G., Paris